CRISES DO HAPPEN

The Royal Navy and Operation Musketeer, Suez 1956

Geoffrey Carter

For
Timothy and Joanna

Published by Maritime Books, Lodge Hill, Liskeard, Cornwall PL14 4EL,
England

Printed and bound by Biddles Ltd, King's Lynn, Norfolk

Contents

Acknowledgements

This study of the Royal Navy at Suez in 1956 arose from my work as a part-time volunteer researcher at the Fleet Air Arm Museum, Yeovilton. In listing material held in a box marked 'Campaigns', I found a folder on Suez. Further investigation revealed that, although the work of the Fleet Air Arm was thoroughly examined in Brian Cull's book, '*Wings over Suez*' and there were already published works on the campaign as a whole, there was no specific naval history, indicating the considerable resources that had to be made available to launch and support the landings at Port Said. Although the operation came to an abrupt halt after only a few days, the Royal Navy's commitment continued after the cease-fire. Throughout the subsequent research, Commander David Hobbs RN and his enthusiastic team at Yeovilton have been most supportive, with advice on sources, and permitting access to the Museum's archives over a period of more than two years. Commander Hobbs kindly agreed to read the manuscript in draft, and give advice from a professional viewpoint. Responsibility for any opinions and conclusions remain mine. Throughout the preparation of this work, my wife has given much practical support as well as positive encouragement in moments of confusion.

Valuable information was received from the following, most of whom were participants in O*peration Musketeer*:*

Lt Cdr T J Andrews RN, Commodore Ian Berry RNR, Lt Cdr Anthony Browne RN, J B Callus, (Lt) Philip Cardew, M P Cocker, Peter Dennerley, (Lt) John Ford, Captain M Fulford-Dobson CVO KStJ JP RN, Captain W E B Godsal RN, Cdr W S de B Griffith RN, Rear Admiral E R Gueritz CB DSO DSC, Lt Cdr John Hard RNR, Captain N Kettlewell RN, Peter Laurie, Ronald Macintyre, (ERA) R McKenzie, Rear Admiral P N Marsden, Peter Miles, Vice Admiral Sir Charles Mills KCB CBE DSC KStJ, Lt Cdr H O'Grady RN, Lt Cdr John Pallot RN, Captain R H M Richardson-Bunbury RN, Lt Cdr C J de C Scott RN, John Ritchie, Captain J Stewart RN, Cdr J Suthers RN, Lt Cdr Peter Wells-Cole RN, Lt Cdr R T Weston RD**RNR, Victor Wickman (Malta).

Acknowledgment must properly be given to the staffs of Royal Marines Museum (Eastney), the Tank Museum (Bovington), the Museum of Army Flying (Middle Wallop), the Imperial War Museum, The National Archives (Kew), The Royal Naval Museum (Portsmouth), and Captain Christopher Page of the Naval Historical Branch (Portsmouth).

GHC 2006

* Naval ranks given in brackets are those held at the time of Operation Musketeer.

The Royal Navy must be ready for the unexpected. A flexible, mobile, balanced force is required to meet both the general-purpose and global nature of maritime tasks.

Dr Eric Grove 1999

Chapter 1

The Political Background

From the moment that the Suez Canal was opened in 1869, its presence dominated Anglo-Egyptian relations. Although at first a wholly French venture, Britain soon bought a stake in the management of the canal by acquiring 44% of the Canal Company shares owned by the Khedive Ismail who was faced with financial problems. The Company did not own the Canal but had a concession that enabled it to operate it until 1968, when everything would revert to Egyptian control. In 1882 British troops landed in Egypt to support the Khedive and so began an occupation that lasted for 74 years. In 1888, following the Convention of Constantinople, Britain assumed overall responsibility for keeping the Canal open to shipping, increasing her control further when Egypt was declared a Protectorate in 1914 after the Khedive had been deposed. In 1936 an Anglo-Egyptian treaty was signed, giving Britain the right to keep military forces in the Canal Zone when the free movement of shipping was threatened. From the actions of successive British governments, it is hard to remember that Egypt was in fact an independent country.

The existence of the Canal assumed particular strategic importance. At a stroke it became a vital route for reinforcements to India and British territories in the Far East. For the Royal Navy it enabled more rapid transfer of ships to locations East of Suez, including the fleet maintained on the China Station. It was even important enough to be included in the calculations leading to the design of British capital ships, so that they could pass through the Canal and so avoid the long voyage round the Cape. Throughout the period between the two World Wars, the British Chiefs of Staff were concerned to maintain the security of the Canal, not only to ensure 'that it shall at all times be free and open in time of war as in time of peace to every vessel of commerce or of war without distinction of flag', but also that it was able to operate in the British national and empire interest. Its importance to the Admiralty was further heightened when considering any threat from Japan, as a fleet might be required to be sent to the Far East. In 1937 it was estimated that this would still take 28 days even if the Suez Canal were used.

As if this were not enough, the recommendation of a Royal Commission on Fuel Oil in 1913 led to the decision that oil would gradually take the place of coal as the source of the Royal Navy's motive power. While Welsh steam coal was 'home grown', oil was not and provision had to be made for its safe supply and storage in large quantities. Because of this, in August 1914 the British Government purchased a controlling share in what was to become the Anglo-Iranian Oil Company. The fuel would be transported in tankers from ports in the Persian Gulf, and their route to Britain would be via the Suez Canal, a vital link.

Following the Balfour Declaration of 1917, whereby the British Government favoured a national home in Palestine for the Jewish people, the situation in the Middle East was further complicated after World War Two by the establishment of the state of Israel, leading to a more or less permanent state of tension with Arab states and, all too often, open hostility.

Colonel Abdul Gamal Nasser became President of Egypt on 23 June 1956. Following an agreement signed in 1954, the last British troops had left Port Said ten days earlier, ending a period of British occupation of Egypt that had lasted for more than seventy years. During several days of celebration, the Egyptian flag was hoisted over Navy House in Port Said, the building that had been the local Royal Navy Headquarters. Events leading directly to the Suez campaign began on 26 July 1956 when President Nasser, in a long and rambling speech, nationalized the Suez Canal and stated that the funds raised from operating the canal would be used to finance the Aswan High Dam. By direct use of the words 'de Lesseps' on fourteen occasions in his speech, he set in motion the immediate occupation of the Suez Canal Company's office. In London, Anthony Eden, who had succeeded Winston Churchill as Prime Minister in 1955, was informed of Colonel Nasser's decision at 2215 and immediately called a meeting of ministers and the Chiefs of Staff. In the absence through illness of the Chairman of the Chiefs of Staff Committee, Marshal of the Royal Air Force Sir William Dickson, Admiral Earl Mountbatten became the senior member. Taking the attitude that 'Nasser must not be allowed to get away with it', the Prime Minister asked if an immediate military response was possible. As First Sea Lord, Earl Mountbatten knew that the Mediterranean Fleet had assembled at Malta to await his inspection. He later claimed that he told the Prime Minister that the fleet could sail eastwards from Malta at speed, pick up Royal Marine Commandos already in Cyprus and proceed to occupy Port Said and the northern access to the Suez Canal. Such a speedy response would take the Egyptians by surprise and pre-empt active opposition from members of the United Nations. Unfortunately, it was immediately clear that, even if the initial assault achieved all that was hoped of it, the small force of Royal Marines Commandos could not be rapidly reinforced before Egyptian resistance stiffened and world opinion hardened. The risk was too great, Earl Mountbatten finally did not recommend it, and the notion was abandoned. Subsequent events were to show how long it would actually take to assemble an assault force and bring it to the enemy shore.[1]

The British government denounced the Egyptian move on the grounds that single government control of the canal was unacceptable. Three Power talks took place between the USA, UK and France which ended on 3 August with an agreement to call an international conference in London. By that time, the British had declared a state of emergency. Some reservists were recalled, but the Royal Navy simply cancelled the departure of men due to leave the service at the end of their careers. While not condoning Nassers's action, the Opposition Labour Party warned that it could not support the use of force unless it was within the Charter of the United Nations. International discussions took place throughout much of August, culminating in the appointment of a committee of five nations under the Australian Prime Minister, Sir Robert Menzies, whose task it was to explain to President Nasser a plan for an International Board to run the canal. Nasser rejected the plan on 9 September and the UK Parliament was recalled from its summer recess to discuss the crisis. An Opposition motion of censure was rejected. On 23 September Britain and France referred the dispute to the Security Council of the United Nations. The Council went into secret session and accepted six principles for the management of the canal, which had been agreed in private between Britain, France and Egypt. The Egyptians later refused to accept a British resolution that an eighteen nation plan already put forward to run the canal corresponded to the requirement of the six principles. By late October, the French and Israelis, later joined by the British, had met secretly near Paris. By the Sevres Protocol, they agreed the sequence of events that would precipitate Anglo-French intervention against Egypt. On 29 October Israel would launch a large scale attack on Egypt, striking through the Sinai peninsula towards the Suez Canal; on 30 October Britain and France would issue an ultimatum to both Israel and Egypt, demanding that both nations withdraw ten miles on either side of the Canal; then, on the expiry of the ultimatum on 31 October, Britain and France would, if necessary, carry out their prepared plan, *Operation Musketeer* Revise. It was expected that Egypt would reject the ultimatum, while Israel, a signatory to the Sevres Protocol, would not. Under its terms, Egypt was required to accept an Anglo-French force positioned to guarantee free passage of shipping through the Canal. Israel agreed not to attack Jordan while engaged in hostilities against Egypt, and Britain agreed not to help Jordan if that country attacked Israel. All the provisions of the protocol were, obviously, to remain very secret.[2]

These events in the Middle East took place at a time of international tension. In the Mediterranean and the Middle East, the British and French were already involved with inter-Arab rivalries and persistent conflict between Arabs and the Israelis: the French supplied Ouragan and Mystere jet aircraft to the latter. For the British, there were already military commitments in dealing with insurgency in Cyprus, while the French, having already lost their colonies in South East Asia, were engaged in a struggle against demands for Algerian independence. The Algerians received support from Colonel Nasser. Of particular importance, the Middle East was a major source of oil, which was vital to the economy of industrial nations. For the British, this oil, like other trade, had to be transported by sea, with the Suez Canal forming a vital route to and from the East.

In global terms, divisions among the permanent members of the United Nations Security Council heightened tension. There were two opposing camps. The Western Democracies of the United States of America, France and Great Britain, anxious to preserve their way of life against the threat from the USSR, increasingly had to acknowledge the dominant influence of the USA with its economic and military strength. They had already formed an Atlantic Alliance with other European countries to establish the North Atlantic Treaty Organisation (NATO). The remaining permanent members of the Council were the USSR and China, both powerful Communist states, with the USSR in particular challenging the USA militarily and seeking to extend its sphere of influence in Europe. Indeed, when much attention in the General Assembly of the United Nations was focussed on the Suez crisis, there came, in the early morning of 4 November, the dramatic announcement on Budapest radio by the Hungarian Prime Minister that Soviet troops had invaded Hungary and were attacking Budapest itself. The two crises now vied for world attention. At this time, the strength of the Red Army was not in doubt, but now Soviet sea power had achieved a status second only to that of the United States. China, a sleeping giant maybe, had already made its presence felt with its intervention in the Korean War, a confrontation which had begun in 1950 and had ended in stalemate and suspicion as recently as 1953. Over all hung the much-feared threat of the atomic bomb.

By 1955, both the USSR and NATO had adopted nuclear strategies, which absorbed a significant proportion of the defence budget on both sides of the Iron Curtain. This strategy significantly distorted the balance of the defence budget in the United Kingdom, whose overall financial predicament was delicate. Although conventional weapons remained dominant in the rival forces, progress towards the deployment of missiles was well advanced. By 1956 the original twelve signatories of the NATO alliance had been joined by Greece and Turkey in the Mediterranean and by the Federal German Republic (West Germany). The addition of Greece and Turkey extended the defence of the southern flank of the Alliance. But still the influence of the USA dominated the alliance and it was recognised that its support would be essential should a situation arise where military action was being considered.

In the late summer of 1956, therefore, the British and French anticipated that US support for their opposition to the nationalisation of the Suez Canal by a perceived dictatorial regime would be forthcoming. But the timing was bad. President Eisenhower was seeking re-election, with Election Day on 6 November. Aged 65, he had already suffered heart attacks, and in his election campaign he had to engage with serious domestic issues as well as international problems. Then, when it emerged that Britain, France and Israel had colluded in secret, keeping their activities from the President, he was angered by the intrigue. He also discovered that, in contravention of a 1950 Tripartite Declaration intended to preserve the status quo in the Middle East, France had supplied Israel with 60 Mystere jets instead of the 24 that had been openly agreed with the Americans. The newly operational American U-2 spy plane, which had discovered the presence of the Mysteres, maintained surveillance over the Eastern Mediterranean, and was soon able to report on the movements of Israeli troops and the build up of British and French forces on Cyprus.

Thus, when the British and French governments sought support from Eisenhower in their dealings with Nasser over the Suez Canal it was not forthcoming. The notion of two of his NATO allies 'going it alone' displeased the US President. He was even more surprised that the British Prime Minister could be encouraged to proceed with the military option when a vote of confidence in the House of Commons was only won by 270 votes to 218. John Foster Dulles, the US Secretary of State, although at times equivocal, advised the President against giving support. Thus, in his determination to unseat Colonel Nasser, Anthony Eden succeeded in alienating those who would have allied themselves to the cause had he pursued what were to them more sensible policies. Many members of the Commonwealth, the Arab States and influential members of the United Nations gathered in opposition. The international political climate, therefore, became an uncomfortable environment in which the armed services had to conduct themselves and put their lives at risk.[3]

As tension increased in the Middle East, the British Chiefs of Staff initiated plans for military action against Egypt. Earlier in 1956, they had already approved plans should war occur with Israel. Known as *Operation Cordage*, any campaign would include the neutralisation of the Israel Air Force, a naval blockade, air attacks against Israeli ground forces and Commando raids on the Israeli Coast. It was anticipated that the campaign would last up to six months before the Israelis would sue for peace.[4] Now, as planning was initiated for a similarly structured campaign against Egypt, there were some misgivings, with General Sir Gerald Templer, Chief of the General Staff and Air Chief Marshal Sir Dermot Boyle, Chief of the Air Staff taking a more hawkish stance than Air Marshal Sir William Dickson, the independent chairman of the Chiefs of Staff Committee, and the First Sea Lord, Earl Mountbatten. From the start it was agreed that there were two possible landing areas in Egypt, at Alexandria or Port Said. Alexandria had the advantages that it was a deep-water port enabling rapid discharge from ocean going ships and advance out of the city could not be easily prevented. Port Said was shallower, lacked the capacity to discharge ships directly to the shore, and attempts to break out could be hindered by the demolition of bridges in key positions. On the other hand, if the preservation of the Canal as an international waterway was a prime objective, then Port Said was the more appropriate landing area. The operation against Egypt was codenamed *Operation Musketeer* and went through several planning stages. Alexandria was first chosen for the landings and 17 September identified as the earliest date the invasion could take place. This date, however, demanded that orders to sail must be given at least six days in advance.[5] Throughout this time the political climate was changing. Lack of support from the United States and mounting world opposition increased doubts about military intervention among members of the Cabinet and the Chiefs of Staff. There was also growing concern over the likelihood of heavy civilian casualties from any aerial and naval bombardment prior to the landings. On 7 September, therefore, the Chiefs of Staff were told to prepare a revised plan, with the landings taking place at Port Said. Air power, combined with diplomatic pressure and psychological warfare, would be employed to overcome the Egyptian will to resist. The Egyptian Air Force was to be destroyed within 48 hours, and every effort would be made, by careful selection of targets, to reduce the risk of civilian casualties. It might even be that the landings, if required at all, would be unopposed. Now that Port Said had become the chosen landing area, the original *Musketeer* forces could still be used, but the ships had to be reloaded to enable them to land their cargoes in a shallow water port. The target date for the new operation, called *Operation Musketeer Revise*, was set for 8 October. Delays in preparation continued, partly due to political indecision and collusion, but also because of the time required to prepare and assemble the invasion force.

Hostilities eventually broke out on 29 October when Israeli forces crossed the Egyptian border and attacked positions in the Sinai desert. Events moved rapidly according to the plan agreed at Sevres with an Anglo-French ultimatum to Egypt and Israel to cease all hostilities. As expected, the ultimatum was accepted by Israel and rejected by Egypt. At a meeting of the Security Council the British and French used their veto twice, once against a US resolution and once against the Soviet Union. Anglo-French military operations against Egypt, described by Anthony Eden as 'a police action', began late on 31 October, as anticipated in the Sevres Protocol. On 2 November the United Nations General Assembly called for a cease-fire, whereupon the British and French laid down conditions. Then on 4 November, the day on which Soviet troops entered Budapest and overthrew the Hungarian government, it was announced that the Egyptians had blocked the Suez Canal. By that time, the Egyptian Air Force had been destroyed and British and French forces were on their way to Port Said. From the date of the nationalisation of the Suez Canal to the first British and French military intervention, three months had elapsed. While military success might still be achieved, the long gestation period virtually guaranteed political failure.

Chapter 2

Planning and Assembling the Forces

The command structure for the *Operation Musketeer Revise* placed a British officer in command of each naval, army and air force contingent with a French deputy. General Sir Charles Keightley GCB GBE DSO was appointed overall Commander–in-Chief of the Allied Forces. His deputy was Vice-Admiral d'Escardre P Barjot, who also commanded all the French forces engaged in the operation. Separate commanders were appointed for each of the three armed services engaged. Lt General Sir Hugh Stockwell KCB KBE DSO commanded the Land Task Force with General Beaufre, commanding the French troops, as his deputy. The Air Task Force Commander was Air Marshal D Barnett CBE DFC with General de Brigade R Brohon as deputy and Commander of the French Air Forces. For the Royal Navy, the CinC Mediterranean was Admiral Sir Guy Grantham GCB CBE DSO. His Flag Officer Second in Command, Mediterranean (FO2) was Vice Admiral M Richmond, who had almost completed his tour of duty in the post. Vice-Admiral Richmond and his staff planned the naval side of *Operation Musketeer* until 24 October, when the Admiral finally left for London. Once there, he took charge of the Allied Forces Headquarters Rear Link at the Ministry of Defence. As the newly appointed FO2, Vice Admiral Durnford Slater took command of the Naval Task Force for *Operation Musketeer*, designated TF 345, only a few days before hostilities began. He hoisted his flag on 26 October. The structure of command of the Naval Task Force was as follows:

TF 345   Vice-Admiral L F Durnford-Slater CB FO2, (Naval Task Force Commander): Deputy, Rear Admiral P Lancelot (in command French Naval Forces). The orders for Task Force 345 stated that it was to be prepared to carry out air opera tions for 30 days if necessary.[1]

TG 345.4   Vice Admiral M L Power CB CBE DSO (Flag Officer Aircraft Carriers)

TG 345.9   Rear Admiral G B Sayer CB DSC (Flag Officer Helicopter Group).

TG 345.5   Rear Admiral D E Holland-Martin DSO DSC* (Flag Officer Support Forces).

TG 345.2   Commodore R deL Brooke DSO DSC* (Commodore Assault Forces)

TG 345.7   Captain J H Walwyn OBE RN (Captain Minesweeping Group)

The Allied Naval Force in the Red Sea, designated TF 324, was commanded by Captain J G Hamilton RN (Senior Officer, Red Sea Group).

Vice-Admiral Robin (Leonard Francis) Durnford-Slater, the Flag Officer appointed to command the British and French naval forces in *Operation Musketeer* was born in 1902. By the time World War II broke out, he had already commanded a destroyer, HMS *Codrington*, and then, during the war he served aboard the aircraft carrier *Hermes* and at HMS *Vernon*. He was Senior Officer of two Escorts Groups and Training Captain on the Staff of the CinC Western Approaches before becoming Director of Underwater Weapons at the Admiralty in Bath. He became Senior Officer 1 Escort Flotilla in the Far East, followed by appointments as Commandant of the School of Amphibious warfare, Captain of the cruiser *Gambia* and Deputy Controller at the Admiralty.   He was then appointed as Commander of the Naval Forces during *Operation Musketeer*.

Known as 'Laughing Boy' because of his serious demeanour, he was nevertheless respected by those who served with him and did not in fact lack a sense of humour. Described by General Beaufre as 'clean shaven, calm, reflective'[2], he was acknowledged as a good listener and a deep thinker. At times apparently reticent, he may well have been a shy man; yet he was quietly efficient, maybe not a conversationalist, but very good on paper. In times of danger he was imperturbable. When Captain Fell arrived at Port Said to work on wreck clearance, he was immediately impressed by Durnford-Slater's style in conducting business and his admiration grew as the Task Force Commander grappled with the constant problems that arose after the cease-fire with the Egyptians and with Lieutenant-General Wheeler, a retired US Engineer Corps officer, appointed by the United Nations to take charge of the clearance operations.[3]

The decision to mount *Operation Musketeer* put an unexpected strain on the command and communications organisation, particularly in the Mediterranean. It also challenged the Royal Navy as a whole to respond effectively whilst still meeting its global commitments. The Fleet of 1956 was still a significant force on the world scene, but it consisted largely of ships built during or very soon after the Second World War. Of the aircraft carriers, *Ark Royal, Eagle, Albion, Bulwark* and *Centaur* all had been completed in the 1950s, but had been laid down during World War Two. Improvements incorporated into their design led to an increase in displacement, and included the angled deck arrangement to allow for the operation of the more powerful and heavier jet aircraft required by the fleet. *Victorious,* with a distinguished war record, was undergoing a major reconstruction. The five carriers of the 'Colossus' class had not been mod-ernised to the same extent as the other carriers, but two of them, *Ocean* and *Theseus,* serving as the Home Fleet Training Squadron, were to fulfil an impor-tant role in the coming operations. Five battleships were in reserve, while the cruiser force, apart from *Superb*, consisted entirely of wartime or pre-war ships. The Daring class large destroyers were relatively new ships, with the Weapons class and the Battles being completed during the period from 1945 to 1948. The large group of 'C' class destroyers included a number of ships completed before the war ended. The anticipated importance of anti-submarine warfare had led to the conversion of many destroyers of wartime construction into anti-submarine frigates. Other frigates described as general-purpose ships, were retained in anti-submarine or anti-aircraft roles.

In the immediate post war period, including the years of the Korean conflict, the Labour government had increased defence spending to the point where it was more than the country could afford. The following Conservative adminis-trations sought to introduce cuts that would enable manpower to be transferred to productive employment, thus alleviating the problem of the balance of pay-ments that had become chronic. The need for new construction was recognised by Viscount Hailsham, the recently appointed First Lord, when he spoke at the Navy League Trafalgar Day Lunch in October 1956. Despite public opinion, which favoured a reduction in expenditure on defence, he concluded:

> "One thing is certain. As long as we remain at peace or in cold or limited war, so long as there is a need to carry our influence from the Falkland Islands to the Far East, over Asia and Africa, from the north of Norway south to Antarctica, so there will be an urgent and indispensable need for a Royal Navy capable of dis-charging its duty."[4]

The Fleet remained committed to a worldwide role. The Home Fleet, in earlier times a major fighting force, was now made up of three cruisers, a fast minelay-er, three Darings, three destroyers and eleven frigates. The flagship of the Home Feet was, surprisingly, the destroyer depot ship *Tyne.* At Portland were the two carriers of the Home Fleet Training Squadron, *Ocean* and *Theseus.* Overseas bases were retained at Singapore, where the Far East Fleet was based, and at Malta, Hong Kong and Simons Town, though the government of Ceylon (Sri Lanka) had decided to close the former base at Trincomalee. The Mediterranean Fleet, soon to be engaged in serious operations against Egypt, had always been a powerful force, and remained so, within the limits imposed by the defence budget. Already, coastal minesweepers were engaged in patrols off Cyprus to prevent the smuggling of arms to insurgents. In March 1956, the frigate *Loch Fada* embarked Archbishop Makarios and other Cypriot leaders, taking them to exile in the Seychelles. Ships of the Mediterranean Fleet performed their tradi-tional humanitarian role in bringing relief to victims of an earthquake in the Lebanon. Smaller forces served in the East Indies, America and West Indies and the South Atlantic. The Royal Navy had, until now, retained a sizeable Reserve Fleet, but it was costly to maintain, and it was announced in the 1956 Naval Estimates that it should be run down.

The tasks set for the Royal Navy in *Operation Musketeer* were first of all to take part in the Allied air offensive aimed at neutralising the Egyptian Air Force, and then to conduct air operations aimed at destroying the Egyptian will to resist. Next, with French naval forces, they were to land Allied Land Forces in Egypt by an assault on Port Said, support them ashore, then to open up and defend Port Said and so enable the Allied Land Forces to achieve a rapid consolidation and build up. The final task was to open the Suez Canal itself to international traffic.[5] The Task Force was told to be prepared to carry out operations for thirty days if necessary.

To achieve these aims, a considerable fleet was assembled. The Headquarters Ship of the Joint Task Force was HMS *Tyne* (Captain J W Bennett DSC RN). The ship would accommodate the three service commanders, Vice-Admiral L F Durnford-Slater, Lieutenant General Sir Hugh Stockwell and Air Marshall D F Barnett, together with their staffs. Built as a destroyer depot ship and completed in 1941, *Tyne* had fulfilled the unlikely role of Flagship of the Home Fleet from 1954 until August 1956. For the present task, she was fitted out for her important communications role, with many of the Royal Navy's Communications Branch making up a large part of the ship's company. These men were supplemented with signallers from the RAF and the Royal Corps of Signals. In due course French communications personnel joined the ship.

The British Aircraft Carrier Task Group, tasked with providing air cover for the operation as well as ground strikes, consisted of *Eagle* (Flag), *Albion* and *Bulwark*. When planning was in its early stages, it was suggested that, after the initial operations were over, *Eagle* and *Bulwark* might disembark their aircraft and become troop carriers, carrying support units to Egypt. The proposal was not pursued.[6] The three ships concentrated at Malta on 24/25 October when Admiral Grantham was ordered to bring them to 72 hours notice, not for operations against Egypt, but for *Operation Cordage* against Israel. It is not surprising, therefore, that there was some confusion as to who the enemy was. Fortunately, the dispositions remained the same, whichever operation was ordered. The Helicopter Group, whose aircraft were to lift Royal Marines Commandos ashore, was made up of the carriers *Ocean* (Flag) and *Theseus*. The First Cruiser Squadron supported the operations, composed at first of *Jamaica* and HMNZS *Royalist*, but when the New Zealand ship was withdrawn for political reasons, *Ceylon* was detached from the Home Fleet, and sailed from Portland, where she was working up. In the Red Sea, *Newfoundland* led TF 324 under Captain Hamilton, being joined by the Daring class ship *Diana*. Five other Daring class ships, *Duchess* (SO), *Decoy*, *Diamond*, *Defender* and *Daring* remained in the Eastern Mediterranean. Also administered by the Flag Officer Flotilla (FOF Med) were the First Destroyer Squadron of *Chieftain*, *Chaplet* and *Chevron*, and the Third Destroyer Squadron of *Armada*, *St Kitts* and *Barfleur*. HMS *Alamein* was the sole representative of the Fourth Destroyer Squadron, the remaining ships undergoing refit, *Agincourt* and *Corunna* at Malta and *Barrosa* at Gibraltar. The Admiralty Pink List for 6 November 1956[7] also lists in the Eastern Mediterranean, *Cavendish*, *Comet* and *Contest* of the Sixth Destroyer Squadron, two ships of the Fifth Frigate squadron, *Whirlwind*, *Wizard*, and all four ships of the Sixth frigate Squadron, *Undine*, *Ursa*, *Ulysses*, and *Urania*. *Crane* and *Modeste* of the Third Frigate Squadron joined Captain Hamilton in the Red Sea. The only British submarine (of the First Submarine Flotilla) to play a part in *Operation Musketeer* was HMS/M *Tudor*. Together with the French submarine *La Creole*, *Tudor* was ordered to carry out Search and Rescue patrols. The Pink List also indicates the large number of Coastal Minesweepers engaged in important operations in the Eastern Mediterranean. There were ships of 104th, 105th and 108th Minesweeping Squadrons with the Minesweeper Support ship *Woodbridge Haven*.

Significantly, many officers and men in the Royal Navy who were shortly to be engaged in *Operation Musketeer* had already seen service in the frontline, either in the Second World War or the Korean War. They had served from the Arctic to the Pacific in all types of ship. Many were already familiar with the Mediterranean and a number of them had experience of Combined Operations, notably the landings in Madagascar, North Africa, Salerno, and the greatest of them all, *Operation Neptune*, Normandy in June 1944. Although this body of experience was of value, the Admiralty still faced difficulties in manning the ships required for possible operations in the Eastern Mediterranean. Its problem stemmed largely from the fact that it was trying to man too large a navy from the resources at its disposal. To meet the crisis now developing, it was found necessary to retain all ratings whose seven-year engagements expired after 1 September 1956. There were frequent drafting changes and the interruption of summer leave, causing disturbance to ratings. Trouble surfaced only in one ship, aboard *Ocean* on 9 October, when a small number of men appeared to be taking part in an unlawful assembly.[8] Their complaints were noted and the assembly dispersed. The demands of *Operation Musketeer* called for some 560 officers and ratings who would have to be drawn from other posts, either at NATO, from shore establishments, the Reserve Fleet, sea trials of ships entering reserve after refit and even from the preservation of the battleship *Vanguard* at Devonport.[9] Some Home Sea Service ships were sent to the Mediterranean. The Communications Branch would be under particular pressure, so much so that 49 Communications Ratings were borrowed from the submarine service. Discharges from the RN by purchase were stopped and a firmer line taken about granting discharges on compassionate grounds. It was decided that priority should be given to the Fleet aircraft carriers, with both *Eagle* and *Bulwark* being given the increases in their ship's companies that were requested.[10]

Captain C P Mills DSC was appointed Chief of Staff to Vice-Admiral Durnford-Slater, having previously served Vice Admiral Richmond in this capacity. By coincidence Captain Mills was aboard HMS *Jamaica* in Alexandria on the day that President Nasser announced the nationalisation of the Canal. He returned to his ship the next day, not knowing the consequences of the Egyptian decision. Although it was hoped that the ship might remain at Alexandria for a while to support the British community in Alexandria, she was in fact ordered to leave for Cyprus immediately. From Cyprus Captain Mills was ordered to London, where, after a meeting with Earl Mountbatten, he began planning for an operation in the Eastern Mediterranean.[11] Work began under Admiral Richmond, based in London, and the planning staff worked in offices under the War Office in Whitehall. Commander E F Gueritz DSC recalled that he had hardly taken up his appointment with the Flag Officer Home Fleet Training Squadron when he was summoned to London. Planning began on the assumption that operations in the Eastern Mediterranean would last for three months. Commander Gueritz was responsible for logistical support to the operation and immediately consulted the Director of Naval Stores with a request for tankers, stores supplies and victuals.[12] Fortunately there was no shortage of tankers, but there was a difficulty in providing an armament supply ship that could carry out transfers at sea. He had two ships that were capable of replenishment in harbour or in sheltered waters, but the only ship capable of transferring ammunition and naval stores to the fleet carriers by RAS (Replenishment at Sea) was RFA *Retainer*. A former cargo and passenger liner, *Retainer* had only been converted in 1954-1955 to a naval storeship. If this vessel were fully employed she could not meet the demands of the three fleet carriers. Commander Gueritz wisely sought a reserve storeship to support RFA *Fort Duquesne*, and was promised part use of *Fort Dunvegan*. The Admiralty signalled to the CinC Mediterranean on 20 October that *Fort Dunvegan* could meet the requirements of the operation and still adhere to her freighting programme.[13] This contingency proved to be well founded when a propeller fell off *Fort Duquesne* at Gibraltar shortly before the operation began, thus delaying her arrival at Port Said.

Provision had to be made to supply water, possibly in open waters. If the army, having landed successfully and established a bridgehead, found that immediate local water supplies were not available, then it would have to be provided by ship. Indeed, interruption of the supply could extend to the Egyptian civilian population and would require assistance from the military authorities. Water was thus provided for the invasion force through tankers. The French cooperated in the provision of water by washing out a wine ship, described by Commander Gueritz as 'a singular act of allied co-operation'.[14] There were also coastal water carriers, such as *Spapool*, accustomed to the distribution of water in harbour.

Once the ships had taken on their stores, ammunition fuel and victuals in anticipation of an operation, they could not be kept waiting indefinitely. Ships carrying transport and equipment would suffer deterioration, for example in batteries, that could prevent vehicles from starting at critical times, and there was always the danger from petrol fumes.

After World War Two operations ranging from small-scale Commando raids to the complexity of the invasion of Normandy (*Operation Overlord*), it might have been assumed that the value of amphibious forces would continue to be recognised and the necessary forces maintained after the war. Indeed, after 1945, the Korean War and sundry smaller-scale operations demonstrated the importance of flexibility and rapidity in response to an emergency, and confirmed the importance of a capability to put a force on the ground anywhere in the world through control of the sea and air. However, in a post war world dominated by two ideologically opposed super-powers with nuclear weapons, the United Kingdom sought to exert influence through an expensive policy of nuclear deterrence. This decision resulted in amphibious warfare assuming a lower priority in the allocation of resources. In fact the United Kingdom had no amphibious capability at all until 1951 when a small force was established in the Mediterranean, based at Malta, but only capable of embarking one Army battalion. The number of landing craft in commission with this force was also small, and the larger number held in reserve at home was elderly and often in poor condition.

By the mid 1950's it was recognised that minor wars might occur even though the threat of a major nuclear confrontation remained. Such possibilities had to be assessed and met when there was heavy pressure on a defence budget that many wished to be reduced. A then recently presented paper '*The Future Role of the Navy*'[15] put a new approach to the Cold War and Limited War and stated that British interests were best served by using amphibious forces based upon an aircraft carrier and a helicopter commando carrier, thus avoiding reliance on overseas shore bases.[16] It was in this climate of change that the sudden requirement to mount an amphibious operation in the Mediterranean arose.

The planners of *Operation Musketeer* had to provide sufficient landing craft to carry out the planned sea assault and sustain it. There already existed at Malta the small Amphibious Warfare Squadron (AWS), consisting of the LSH (Landing Ship Headquarters) *Meon*, the *ML 2583*, the LST(A) (Landing Ship Tank) *Reggio* and *Striker* and the LCT(8) (Landing Craft Tank) *Bastion* and *Redoubt*. Of the ships that must be brought forward from reserve, some were found to be in better condition than others.[17] The LST *Suvla*, for example, was selected rather than *Battler* because the former was in better condition and carried a Type 268 radar and VHF. Finally, four ships, already at Malta, were commissioned from reserve: LST(A) *Anzio*, LST(3) *Lofoten* and two LCT(8) *Citadel* and *Portcullis*. In addition, 37 LCA (Assault Landing Craft), which were carried aboard and launched from the LST were brought forward from reserve in Malta and the UK, while 18 LVT (Landing Vehicles Tracked) came from Cambridge, where they had been held in reserve. Manning presented a problem, met by a reduction in dead ships' crews of the reserve ships at Malta, the suspension of leadership courses at HMS *Ricasoli* (Malta), and by transferring some supernumerary ratings from other ships. From Supplementary Reserve in the Clyde, via Devonport, came LSTs *Puncher*, *Salerno*, *Suvla*, *Ravager*, all at 28 days notice and all overdue for refit. They were all ordered forward to Devonport on 2nd and 3rd August, but did not reach Malta until early September, with *Puncher*, carrying the 6th Royal Tank Regiment HQ on board, being the last to arrive on 16 September. When Lt Cdr John Pallot joined LST *Salerno* on the north side of the Clyde from Greenock, the ship was almost ready to sail. Although the steering gear broke down in the Irish Sea, the ship made Devonport successfully, allowing dockyard workers to begin their hammering, drilling and welding.[18] On arrival, the loading of the LST required careful attention and understanding of the ship's trim when the time came to unload. Once the tanks had arrived at Devonport, loading normally took between two and three hours. In *Salerno*, the tanks of C Squadron 6 Royal Tank Regiment were loaded quickly. Some delay was due to the upper deck space forward of the bridge being occupied by four LCA, this perhaps being the reason why one tank and two 3-ton trucks could not be taken on board. The arrival of the Centurion tanks for loading was delayed. They could not be moved by train, nor were they permitted to travel by road under their own power. There were no military tank transporters available, so movement depended upon Pickfords, a trades union manned company which made the delivery of the tanks to the ports ' expensive, inconvenient, slow and wasteful'.[19] Further irritation was caused when a county surveyor would not permit the tanks be unloaded onto the road, even when the transporters were unable to negotiate hills. When permission was later granted it was found that the tanks did little damage to the road surface.[20] As a result, the journeys took from five to seven days instead of two to three. On her departure on 2 September, *Salerno* met a strengthening wind and rising sea, so that for two days the ship rolled, on occasion, through 30 degrees each way with intervals of 7 seconds. Fortunately the weather cleared well before the ship reached Malta on 11 September.[21]

To augment the force of Tank Landing Craft, LCT(8) *Parapet, Counterguard, Sallyport* and *Buttress* sailed from the United Kingdom together with *Rampart*, which was normally in commission in home waters. Those carrying tanks could complete loading from berthing in about 1 hour 35 minutes. They arrived in Malta at the end of August. Some of the LCA, due to carry the assault troops onto the beaches, were in a particularly poor state. Preparation, however, did not end with the arrival of these ships at Malta. They still had to be brought 'to a fit state of both material and training to carry out the operation'.[22] This was not achieved until the end of September and involved Commodore R deL Brooke, the Commodore AWS, being away from planning meetings for long periods while he 'licked his Squadron into shape.'[23] Most of his ships had been brought out of reserve and training had to start largely from first principles. While they and their crews might have been speedily commissioned and made ready for sea, this did not mean they were fit to take part in operations. Defects had to be remedied, alterations made and attention paid to habitability without diluting the training programme. Commodore Brooke's assessment was that, although craft and crews were ready on the day, they could not achieve 'Rolls-Royce standards'.[24]

Plans to use more LST met with difficulty. Up to 12 Admiralty LST were to be prepared, but this lasted so long into November that they took little part in operations.[25] Seven LST on charter to the Atlantic Steam Navigation Company, known as 'Bustard boats' were obtained, plus seven War Department vessels of the 'Gentleman' class.

The troops selected to carry out the initial seaborne assault were drawn from the 3rd Commando Brigade Royal Marines, commanded by Brigadier R W Madoc OBE ADC. 40 and 45 Commandos were ordered to Malta from Cyprus early in August, but 42 Commando, then a training unit, sailed out from the United Kingdom in the trials cruiser *Cumberland*. They began training with the Amphibious Warfare Squadron as well as co-operating with the tanks of the 6th Royal Tank Regiment. In anticipation of street fighting, they underwent training in derelict buildings near St George's barracks on Malta, where they were stationed.[26] 45 Commando subsequently embarked in the carriers *Theseus* and *Ocean*. They would be air lifted ashore by helicopters of 845 Squadron Fleet Air Arm, and by the combined Army and RAF helicopters of the Joint Helicopter Unit. Earlier, in early August, the carriers *Ocean* and *Theseus* had sailed to Cyprus with parachute troop reinforcements for 16th Parachute Brigade Group, and gunners, giving a total military force of some 2000 men in each ship.

Although the Royal Navy made by far the major contribution of British assault force, the Army sought to add to this from its much more limited resources. No 76 Company RASC (LCT) was formed at Yeovil to operate army Landing Craft.

Difficulties in manning were met by asking for volunteers among civilian personnel. This enabled the army to send three LCT, *Arromanches*, carrying vehicles and stores, and LCT Mk IV *L 403* and *L 408* which could transport vehicles, stores and composite rations. They proceeded in convoy to Malta and on to Famagusta.[27]

A Requisition Ship Order was issued on 3 August, by which the Government could 'requisition for Her Majesty's Service any British ship and anything aboard such ship wherever she might be'.[28] Plans were made for 18 cargo ships of the 'Liberty' type to be taken over, with loading first due to start on 7 August, though the date was soon put back. Three coasters were also need to carry cased petrol. By 7 October 81 ships had been requisitioned, 32 of these had subsequently been released (15 unused), and 49 were still on requisition. For troop carrying, the liner *New Australia* was withdrawn from the migrant service under an agreement with the Australian government. With *Asturias* and *Dilwara*, she embarked troops at Southampton and sailed on 1 November, *Empire Fowey* having sailed the previous day.[29] The voyage to Port Said lasted twelve days. At about the same time as the troopships sailed, so store ships and coasters departed from harbours between Milford Haven and Tilbury. Eight ships sailed on 1 November, followed by 9 the next day, 3 on 5 November and 5 on 6 November.[30]

For this 'limited war', an overwhelming force was assembled, based on an assessment of Egyptian opposition that could be strengthened by the presence of Soviet bloc personnel manning Soviet equipment. The Royal Navy with its Mediterranean Fleet was a formidable force in itself, and it was already in the area. But it needed reinforcement to sustain its air offensive and to lift equipment and troops for the landing. The two carriers *Theseus* and *Ocean* could move at high speed to the scene. Their helicopters, though small in number and hastily adapted to lift troops ashore, were capable of a rapid response. But the ships required for the sea assault were elderly and too slow. Their voyage would last six days. In any case they could not be kept at sea for more than 7-8 days without diverting to Cyprus and if this happened, the convoys from Cyprus to Port Said would take a further 36 hours. The Royal Air Force could mount a force of more than 100 bombers together with 48 Venoms, 24 Hunters and 36 French F84F fighters. With the British and French carrier borne squadrons, Air Marshal Barnett could combat the Egyptian Air Force, albeit with its modern Russian MiGs and Ilyushins plus more elderly British built Meteors and Vampires.[31] The army raised the equivalent of two British and two French divisions with further reinforcement from British Forces in Germany and French divisions from France should they be required.[32]

The situation as hostilities were about to begin was complicated. Collusion between the United Kingdom, France and Israel placed the armed services in a position, which, if disclosed, would be embarrassing. The ultimatum presented to Egypt and Israel to withdraw their forces seemed to be a move to bring about peace. The intention was to enable Israel to accept the ultimatum but ensure an Egyptian rejection, thus precipitating a military intervention. But such a rejection could not be assumed. Timing was all-important. Action should follow as soon as possible after the ultimatum expired. Air attacks on Egyptian airfields could begin at once, but the slow military convoys from Malta would take six days to complete the voyage to Port Said and would have to sail well before the ultimatum expired. The major weakness of the plan was that, with a desire to avoid military risk, the build up of substantial force took too long and allowed world wide political opinion to harden against the enterprise. A rapid response force of airborne troops and naval amphibious forces deployed to take the Canal could almost certainly have achieved success. At the time, appropriate troops and equipment were not available. While the motto of the SAS 'Who dares wins' might have been appropriate for the Suez venture, the Allies regrettably could not dare. The British, holding all the senior commands, were cautious, an approach increasingly reinforced by their political masters. The French, subordinate in command, wished to be less inhibited and were prepared to be more aggressive, most notably through their well-led and well-equipped parachute troops.

Chapter 3

The Carriers Strike

Throughout *Operation Musketeer* it was certain that a major responsibility would fall upon the aircraft carriers *Eagle*, *Albion*, *Bulwark* and their air groups. The force assembled had to be sufficient to meet likely contingencies. As early as July 1956, the CinC Mediterranean had informed the Admiralty that if operations were to be undertaken against Egypt, two carriers would be inadequate against the Egyptian Air Force, especially as RAF fighters based in Cyprus would be out of effective range. At the same time he observed, mistakenly as it turned out:

> I imagine we should never attempt to do this without American carriers working with us.[1]

The timing of the operation was somewhat unfortunate, for the Royal Navy was in the process of converting its carriers to have angled decks, a necessary provision if they were to be able to operate the new generation of jet aircraft. In the autumn of 1956, although five British carriers had angled decks, only two were in commission. *Ark Royal* was undergoing an extended refit at Devonport and *Centaur* was being modernised. *Albion*, although under refit at Portsmouth, was due to rejoin the fleet in October. Of the remaining two carriers, only *Eagle* was in full commission and worked up, with *Bulwark* engaged in trials and training and with no air group on board.

The aircraft carrier force to carry out *Operation Musketeer* was eventually formed under the command of Vice Admiral M L 'Lofty' Power CB, CBE DSO*. He joined the Royal Navy in 1917 and spent his early career in submarines. When war broke out in 1939, however, he was the highly regarded Staff Officer (Operations) to the CinC Mediterranean, Admiral Sir Andrew Cunningham. After a period in command of the destroyer *Opportune* on Russian convoys, he returned to the Mediterranean in time to aid in the planning of landings in North Africa, Sicily, Italy and Anzio. At the time of the landings in Normandy in June 1944, he commanded the 26th Destroyer Flotilla in *Kempenfelt*, followed by command of the destroyer *Myngs* in winter operations off Norway. After the European war ended, he moved to the Far East, once more leading the 26th Destroyer Flotilla, this time in *Saumarez* throughout the action leading to the destruction of the Japanese cruiser *Haguro*. Vice Admiral Power was, therefore, an officer of very considerable wartime experience who had earned high praise both as a Staff Officer and as a destroyer commander in action. After the war he was briefly Director of Plans at the Admiralty, served on the staff of the Joint Service Staff College and was commander of the naval base at Portland. He then became Flag Captain to the CinC Home Fleet (Admiral Sir Philip Vian), followed by Chief of Staff to the CinC Mediterranean, Earl Mountbatten of Burma. Before becoming Flag Officer Aircraft carriers in 1956, he was on the directing staff of the Imperial Defence College.

In July 1956 HMS *Eagle* (Captain H C D Maclean DSC RN) was the only British aircraft carrier in the Mediterranean. Over the next two months she was joined by *Bulwark* (Captain J M Villiers OBE RN) on 7 August and *Albion* (Captain R M Smeeton MBE RN) on 17 September.[2] Earlier in 1956, *Albion* had carried out training exercises with Commonwealth Navies in the Far East, returning to Portsmouth in May for refit, only to be commissioned in a hurry in order to sail for the Mediterranean on 15 September. A pilot in 802 Squadron joining *Albion* described how morale was high and there was confidence in their realistic training. All the squadron were bachelors apart from the Commanding Officer and the Senior Pilot. They all saw themselves as 'carefree young men, thrilled with our luck to be doing what we had always wanted to do, flying a fighter aircraft in a front line squadron'. But experience had already taught them that there was a darker side to life in the Fleet Air Arm, when accidents claimed the lives of colleagues. For 802 Squadron and the other squadrons aboard *Albion*, a period of intense work-up followed.

Bulwark had been a trials and training carrier until recalled to Portsmouth prior to sailing for Gibraltar. Once in the Mediterranean and especially in early September, she engaged in a period of intensive exercises that presumed an air offensive against ground targets and support for an amphibious landing. Exercises were carried out with the Carrier Borne Ground Liaison Section (Ceeballs), whose task it was to talk the aircrew onto their target, or, once ashore, to identify targets by radio or arrows marked on the ground. The speed of attack demanded practice to build confidence between pilot and controller. Flying included pre-dawn launches and ground attack exercises, spotting for the cruiser *Jamaica* (Captain A D Lennox-Conynham RN), and the minelayer *Apollo* (Captain F B P Brayne-Nicholls DSC), while *Apollo's* sister ship *Manxman* (Captain D S Tibbits DSC RN) towed a target for strafing with 20mm cannon. Amphibious assault exercises were also carried out, with the French cruiser *Georges Leygues* included in the force. At the time, naval commanders were still uncertain who the enemy might be; both Israel and Egypt were possible opponents. For the operations ahead the squadrons embarked were:

Eagle	830 Squadron	9 Westland Wyvern S4
	892 Squadron	8 de Havilland Sea Venom FAW21
	893 Squadron	9 de Havilland Sea Venom FAW21
	897 Squadron	12 Hawker Sea Hawk FGA6
	899 Squadron	12 Hawker Sea Hawk FGA6
	849 Squadron	4 Douglas Skyraider AEW1 (A Flight)

Bulwark	804 Squadron	10 Hawker Sea Hawk FGA6
	810 Squadron	10 Hawker Sea Hawk FGA4
	895 Squadron	10 Hawker Sea Hawk FB3
	Ship's Flight	2 Grumman Avenger AS5
Albion	800 Squadron	9 Hawker Sea Hawk FGA4
	802 Squadron	10 Hawker Sea HawkFB3
	809 Squadron	8 de Havilland Sea Venom FAW21
	849 Squadron	4 Douglas Skyraider AEW1 (C Flight)

To sustain operations *Eagle* carried 28 Sea Hawk pilots, 17 crew for the Sea Venoms and 12 pilots for the Wyverns. *Albion*'s 19 Sea Hawks had 24 pilots, with 9 crew for the Sea Venoms and 5 crew for the 4 Skyraiders; *Bulwark* is listed as having 32 pilots for her 30 Sea Hawks.[3]

The Sea Hawk was a popular aircraft with those who flew it, being described by Lt Philip Cardew of 899 Squadron as a 'beautifully built little jet that was particularly easy to fly'. It was however a sub-sonic machine, having entered service in 1953. It was armed with four 20-mm guns in the fuselage, 160 rounds per gun and could carry 3-inch rocket projectiles mounted beneath the wings. In *Operation Musketeer* the Sea Hawks actually carried between four and eight rockets. The Sea Venom was also sub-sonic, but it was an all weather fighter with ground attack capability and carried a crew of two. It, too had four 20–mm guns, 140 rounds per gun, and in this operation normally carried a load of four rocket projectiles. The Wyvern, though popular with its pilots as a stable platform with good visibility, was, and always had been, an unreliable aircraft that had suffered a long period of development, largely due to its unsatisfactory turboprop engine and propeller control unit. Although it could carry a considerable weight of bombs and rockets, it could not at first be risked on targets too far inland in case high performance Egyptian fighters were deployed against it. Its four 20-mm guns were mounted in the wings, 240 rounds per gun, and it also could carry between eight and sixteen rockets, and a single bomb on some sorties.[4] It was withdrawn from service in 1958. The American built Douglas Skyraider could carry a heavy load of radar equipment, and although in the coming operation it carried out a variety of tasks, its primary value was as an airborne early warning radar picket. The two elderly Grumman Avengers carried aboard *Bulwark* had an anti-submarine capability. They were among the last of their type to be supplied to the Fleet Air Arm before conversion to the Fairey Gannet. In addition to the fixed wing aircraft, each carrier operated a Search and Rescue (SAR) Helicopter Flight. *Eagle* and *Albion* carried the Westland Whirlwind HAR3, while *Bulwark* carried the older Westland Dragonfly. To increase the offensive capability of her aircraft in the coming amphibious operation, and in the absence of a serious submarine threat, *Eagle* had replaced 812 Squadron's Fairey Gannets with the de Havilland Sea Venoms of 893 Squadron.

The three fleet aircraft carriers concentrated at Malta on 24 October. They had already carried out exercises together to ensure that they could launch and recover their aircraft in a hostile environment. An exercise in early October found all three carriers involved in a full scale anti submarine exercise with ten escorts and the fast minelayer *Manxman*. The screen was placed round the circumference of a seven-mile circle, each escort having an allotted arc in which she could manoeuvre to hunt submarines. Each of the three carriers was given a sector within the circle.[5] On the morning of 29 October, earlier than scheduled, they sailed from Malta, apparently to carry out *Exercise Boathook*, a communications exercise with Allied Forces Headquarters, Cyprus. *Eagle*, *Albion* and *Bulwark* were joined by two cruisers, the New Zealand cruiser HMNZS *Royalist* (Captain P Phipps RNZN) on 30 October and *Jamaica* (Captain A D Lenox-Conynham RN) the following day. The destroyer screen was commanded by Captain H G H Austin DSO in the Daring class ship *Duchess* with her sister ship *Diamond*, and the Battle class destroyers *Barfleur*, *St Kitts* and *Armada*. HMS *Decoy* and *Alamein* joined on 31 October, and like the other ships, remained with the carriers until detached on 4 November to escort and support the advancing assault convoys. All the ships were under the overall command of the Flag Officer Aircraft Carriers. The fast anti-submarine frigate *Ursa* remained with the carriers throughout the operation, but *Daring* and *Defender* joined for one day on 2 November. Another anti-submarine frigate, *Whirlwind*, did not join until 7 November, after the cease-fire.[6]

The presence of the single Commonwealth ship *Royalist* as Part of Vice Admiral Power's Task Group became somewhat controversial. Her ship's company had brought the cruiser *Bellona* back from New Zealand to the United Kingdom in 1955, and then transferred to *Royalist*. Having recently completed a refit, she now had a new bridge and fire control system as well as lattice masts and had joined the Mediterranean Fleet in July 1956 for training. There seems little doubt that all on board would have welcomed the chance to be involved in *Operation Musketeer*, and this seemed at first to be likely. However, the Prime Minister of New Zealand, Sidney Holland, although at first supportive of the British and French action, soon became less enthusiastic as political opposition mounted. On 18 August, having been asked if *Royalist* could be used for bombardment and anti-aircraft defence, the Admiralty was able to signal to Admiral Grantham that, 'The Prime Minister of New Zealand has agreed that plans may proceed on the assumption that, subject to his final decision at the time, *Royalist* may be used'.[7] Holland was anxious however that the offer should not be made known, and even went so far as to state that, if challenged, he would deny it. A memo from the British Prime Minister on 18 September made clear the value of the extra fire-power *Royalist* would bring to the Fleet, describing the cruiser as having the best anti-aircraft armament of all the British forces in the Mediterranean. With the ships likely to be at sea for a long period, air attacks could be the most serious danger to the naval forces. While Holland agreed that the ship was a valuable asset, he remained concerned at the loss of public support in New Zealand should she become involved in the Anglo-French military venture. For the ship's company, the prospect of their ship being withdrawn at a late stage, with action imminent, was regarded as 'humiliating'. At first, *Royalist* stayed with the fleet but was ordered not to take part in any operations. Had the Egyptian Air Force threatened to attack the fleet, her position would have been difficult. She was on station as a radar picket 30 miles south of the fleet, and would either have had to break away, or, more likely, assuming that she herself was under attack, would have opened fire. In fact, no such air attack took place and *Royalist* was detached from the Carrier Group with *Albion* late on 2 November, and headed north to the Underway Replenishment Group.[8] When Egyptian air attacks on the Fleet failed to materialise, Prime Minister Holland was able to express relief and indicate that now would be an appropriate time for the ship to be sent home. She then proceeded to Malta, and on to Auckland by way of the Cape. In his report, Vice Admiral Power stated that he did not know whether the New Zealand government would allow *Royalist* to take part in the operation, and that is why he detached her northward 'much to her chagrin'. The British cruiser *Jamaica* took her place in the screen.[9]

A public announcement came in a later answer to a House of Commons Parliamentary question, when it was stated that it 'was agreed between Her Majesty's Government and the New Zealand Government that *Royalist* should not be operationally committed'.[10]

This was not the end of the matter. In 2003 the New Zealand government acknowledged that *Royalist* had been involved in a theatre of military operations, and the ship's company became entitled to a medal to commemorate the Suez operation. This action was in response to the lobbying of the RSA (Returned Services Association), and appears to accept that the New Zealand ship was in fact engaged in the war. There is little doubt that *Royalist* would have been allowed to remain with the Task Group throughout *Operation Musketeer* if the British and French action had received international support, or if the New Zealand Prime Minister had held firm to his original commitment.

As the Carrier Group headed eastwards, the ships were not sailing for *Exercise Boathook* at all, but were already on their way to begin operations against Egypt, if and when the Commander in Chief of the Allied Forces gave the order. This first day at sea was a day of low cloud, at times down to 1200 feet, with visibility falling at times to zero in storms. It was also on this day that an event occurred aboard *Eagle* that could have had grave consequences for the operational efficiency of that ship, when a structural failure of the starboard catapult caused the loss of a Sea Hawk. The pilot, Lieutenant L E Middleton, was saved, although his 'bone dome' was cracked when he struck the side of the carrier after escaping from the cockpit. He must have wondered what else the fates had in store, as this was the third crash he had survived during this one commission, having first suffered a 'flame out' in July, and then had his aircraft catch fire when being launched by catapult in September. The starboard catapult remained unserviceable for the whole of *Operation Musketeer*, leaving *Eagle* dependent on the port catapult alone to launch its strike aircraft and thus seriously affecting the rate at which they could operate. The inadequacy of the hydraulic catapults fitted to the three carriers needs some explanation.

HMS *Eagle* was fitted with two catapults of BH5 design. The BH5 had been subjected to a comprehensive series of trials at the Royal Aircraft Establishment, Farnborough (RAE), before the ship was finally accepted into service. These included flying trials to test the catapult's suitability for launching aircraft presently serving in the Fleet. The report was published in April 1952. It stated that the trials, though successful, had been developed to suit such aircraft as the Supermarine Attacker, the first jet fighter to serve in Fleet Air Arm squadrons, and were therefore less than ideal for older aircraft. Of the gas turbine aircraft, the Sea Vampire and Attacker were included in the trials, but the Sea Hawk and the propeller-driven Wyvern, originally intended to be included, were not in fact available. The catapult had been adapted at the RAE to launch the gas turbine aircraft at the maximum possible speed, and no trouble had been experienced with the Attacker, which was described as the only high perform-ance aircraft tested. The initial design performance of the catapult was 30,000 lbs at 75 knots, but this was uprated to 30,000 lbs at 82.5 knots before being fit-ted to the ship. The report concluded:

> Catapults. . . . . . fitted in HMS *Eagle* are suitable for catapulting the existing range of naval aircraft and for those which are likely to be sent to the ship in the near future. . Taken all round, the performance characteristics of the BH5 cata-pult seem to be a reasonable compromise between the needs of the higher per-formance aircraft now coming into service and the necessity to be able to launch the existing range of naval aircraft.[11]

On the day the mishap occurred, the Flag Officer Aircraft Carriers signalled to the CinC Mediterranean that the damage to *Eagle*'s catapult 'would reduce *Eagle*'s effort to 84 offensive and 60 CAP sorties per day'.[12] Clearly the arrival of the more powerful steam catapult was urgently awaited, a matter reinforced later in the campaign when, on 4 November *Bulwark*'s port catapult started to fail, followed later in the month by the failure of the starboard accelerator rope. *Albion*'s catapults, too, gave cause for anxiety.

As the Carrier Group continued at high speed into the Eastern Mediterranean, there was intense activity in each ship to prepare for action. Morale amongst the carrier squadrons was high. For many it would be their first experience of being shot at, but they were confident in the quality of their training. Threats had to be considered possible from 'unknown or hostile' submarines in or near Egyptian waters, but this was considered 'slight'.[13] The Egyptian Navy's destroyers and coastal craft might attack the carriers with torpedoes accepting heavy losses. Exercises to counter a surface threat were carried out, including 'Gloworm' seri-als by the Sea Venom night fighters. This night exercise involved a low level approach to the target. The leading aircraft drew ahead of the others, then pulled up to fire a Gloworm 3-inch rocket which released a parachute flare to illumi-nate the target, while the aircraft completed a loop or circuit to come in again and complete its attack. But it was the Egyptian Air Force rather than the Egyptian Navy that presented the more serious threat from a significant number of modern aircraft, unless they could be neutralised while on the ground.

Eagle was proceeding at 26 knots for much of the day and night of 30 October, causing such vibration that sleep was difficult. Flying was limited to a night launch, pre-dawn form up and strike with one other detail of four aircraft. Two of *Eagle*'s Skyraiders carried out anti-submarine patrols while the remaining two machines searched for an unidentified fleet that appeared on the plot some 200 miles away. This emerged as the French aircraft carrier squadron of *Arromanches* (ex-HMS *Colossus*) and *La Fayette*, (the ex-USS *Langley*), with five destroyers. *Arromanches* had on board 36 Chance Vought Corsair F4U pro-peller driven aircraft, while *La Fayette* carried 10 Grumman Avenger TBM-3.

In addition, each ship carried two HUP-2 helicopters. The French ships had sailed from North African ports, and, like the British Task Force, refuelled off Crete, but from French tankers. The opportunity was taken to exchange Liaison Officers between the two carrier groups. The British carrier group arrived in the Eastern Mediterranean on 31 October, at which time the French came under the operational control of Vice Admiral Power. Thus TG 345 was activated, though the French group had its own area of operations because of differences in operational speeds.[14]

There remained uncertainty about when, or even if, operations against Egypt would begin, so much so that CinC Mediterranean signalled to Vice Admiral Power that he had 'no - repeat no - information other than that on BBC broadcasts'. He concluded, 'Do not start briefing yet'. However, with no further flying that day, it seems that Royal Navy aircrew were briefed, being informed of possible targets, tasks and opposition. They were kitted out with extra equipment to add to the normal 'bone dome', oxygen mask and 'Mae West'. This consisted of Talk and Listen equipment that transmitted on the International Distress Frequency, a water bottle with 1.5 pints of water, a service revolver with 24 rounds of ammunition and probably a knife too. Since it was possible that ejection from their aircraft might be made over land, flying boots or strong shoes were to be worn. Khaki shirts and trousers, with secreted escape and evasion equipment, completed their kit. During the day, ground crews painted their aircraft with distinctive black and yellow stripes, while arming parties prepared rockets, bombs and 20mm ammunition.[15] Vice Admiral Durnford-Slater's orders to Vice Admiral Power were clear; 'Black and yellow stripes are to be painted on your aircraft by the time you reach the operations area'. Aboard the carriers, ready use lockers were filled with ammunition for AA gun mountings and 4.5-inch turrets.

Later in the day, the three British carriers refuelled from the RFA *Olna*. The screen rejoined and course was set for the position from which a pre-dawn launch might be made if hostilities were about to begin. A signal from General Keightley, Commander-in-Chief Allied Forces, saying 'No action will be taken by you tonight 30/31 October' caused Vice Admiral Power some surprise, as he had never expected to be engaged in a night action anyway.[16] The signal merely added to a situation that the Vice Admiral described as 'baffling even to one extensively trained in Joint Service Operations'. The next day, however, would at last see the implementation of *Operation Musketeer*.

Operational orders had already been issued to both groups. From D-Day minus 3 (D-3) until D-Day plus 4(D+4) all air operations were directed by Air Marshal Denis Barnett, the Officer Commanding all air operations, based at Episcopi, Cyprus. His orders to CTG 345.4 were issued in a daily directive in which he laid down 'the overall aim, broad tasks and priorities' while at the same time giving the Flag Officer Aircraft Carriers 'maximum freedom of action'. Later in the campaign, from D+4 to D+6, Air Marshall Barnett conducted operations from HMS *Tyne*.[17] Early in the morning, while still dark, navigation lights were switched off and the ships began to zigzag, then during the day Skyraiders again carried out patrols, this time of local and inshore waters, spotting at least one frigate and a fast motor vessel, both presumed to be Egyptian. A Combat

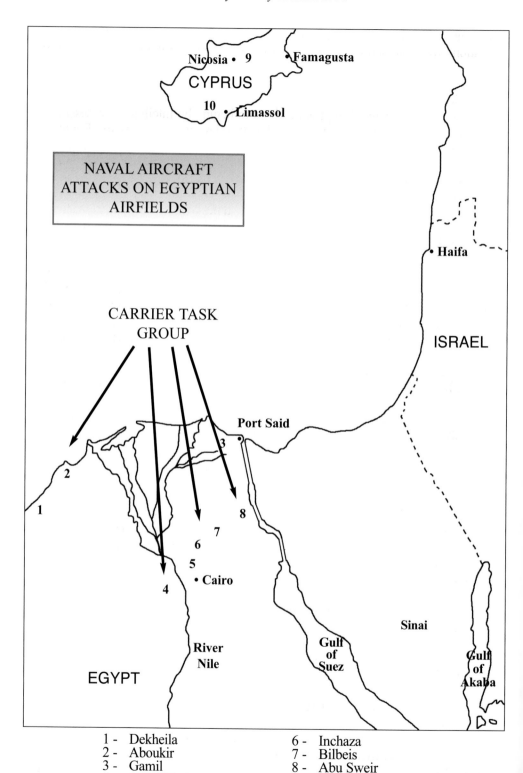

NAVAL AIRCRAFT ATTACKS ON EGYPTIAN AIRFIELDS

CYPRUS

Nicosia • 9   • Famagusta

10 • Limassol

• Haifa

CARRIER TASK GROUP

ISRAEL

Port Said

3

2

1

8

7

6

5

4

• Cairo

Sinai

Gulf of Suez

Gulf of Akaba

River Nile

EGYPT

1 -	Dekheila	6 -	Inchaza
2 -	Aboukir	7 -	Bilbeis
3 -	Gamil	8 -	Abu Sweir
4 -	Cairo West	9 -	Tymbou (Fr)
5 -	Almaza	10 -	Akrotiri (RAF)

Air Patrol (CAP) was maintained over the force. Even so the call to Action Stations was sounded on a number of occasions during the day when aircraft were sighted on radar, though no threat developed. Later radar plots showed more activity as Allied aircraft from Cyprus headed south towards Egypt on their first raids to destroy the Egyptian Air Force on the ground.

As operations against Egypt were about to begin, the Intelligence assessment of the opposing forces became immediately relevant. As far as the Egyptian Navy was concerned, it was judged that morale was low compared with the Air Force and the Army. The Navy had never been represented in the Egyptian Council of Revolutionary Command, and there had been a purge of officers, regarded as Royalist, after the formation of the Revolutionary Corps in 1952. There was some dissatisfaction in ships' companies over an increase in sea time, yet the elite frogman unit had been inactive. The Egyptian ships were regarded as unreliable, although newer Russian Skory class destroyers and Motor Torpedo Boats from Yugoslavia were likely to be more efficient. The Allied naval forces had to take the MTB threat seriously and must reckon on mines being laid in the entrances and approaches to Port Said and the Canal itself. Mining off Malta and Cyprus was not ruled out. Submarines were known to have been ordered from the Soviet Bloc, but probably not delivered. If they were to be present, it was thought unlikely that Egyptian crews would be sufficiently trained to operate them, but if Soviet or Polish 'volunteers' manned them, there were serious political implications. On 30 August 1956 the Director of Naval Intelligence (DNI) assessment was that Egypt had no patrol submarines:-

> Should any be delivered in the near future, we should become aware. They are unlikely to be delivered and would be very inefficient by our standards. It is unlikely but possible that up to four midget submarines may have been delivered to Egypt.[18]

He concluded that any Russian submarines in the area would be unlikely to shadow and report the Allied forces. Close watch was kept on any submarine movements likely to influence events. When the Polish submarine *M107*, escorted by a Polish tanker, entered the Mediterranean on 1 November, and was believed to be en route for Alexandria to join the Egyptian Navy, it was tracked by Allied aircraft until, at 1928Z the ships reversed course and increased speed. They continued to be tracked until they entered the North Sea.[19] The possible response to the presence of a submarine was the subject of much signalling before operations began. The rules of engagement must be established. A submerged submarine might be Egyptian, but could also be a Soviet vessel or part of the US Sixth Fleet. The risk of an international incident that might inflame an already delicate political situation was ever present. Signals expressed the need for caution.

The Egyptian Air Force posed a more immediate threat to the Task Groups. It was in the process of equipping its first line squadrons with Soviet Bloc aircraft. Although the MiG-15 and MiG-17 fighters and Ilyushin Il-28 bombers were of high performance, flying training was incomplete and the squadrons were reckoned to lack technically qualified ground crews. The Intelligence assessment concluded that, unless foreign crews manned these aircraft, they were unlikely to be effective in a tactical role. General Keightley estimated that his forces faced 80 MiG-15s, 45 Il-28 bombers, plus 25 Meteors and 57 Vampires supplied by the British. In addition he believed there were some 200 training, communication and transport aircraft. These figures did not include forces known to be engaged with the Israelis in Sinai.[20]

Vice Admiral Power's appreciation was that, at least in the initial phase of the operation, the most likely danger would be from the air, with attacks by surface ships or submarines forming a lesser threat. If the new high performance aircraft should attack his ships and if well-trained crews manned them, he recognised that some of them might break through the Combat Air Patrols maintained from the carriers.

The three Royal Navy aircraft carriers took up positions some 60 miles off the Egyptian coast, a distance that allowed their air strikes to be given radar cover. Their Underway Replenishment Group was stationed 30 miles to the north. For pre-dawn operations each carrier had its own screening ships for anti-aircraft defence or acting as planeguard. For other operations each carrier operated independently with its own support ships, and was allotted a sector within a circle of 7 miles, a formation already practised. Thus, when appropriate, the ships could fly their aircraft in staggered cycles, whether on strikes, CAP or Cabranks; the last composed of standing air patrols of ground attack aircraft, ready when called upon to strike immediately in support the troops on the ground.

The Royal Air Force prepared for the coming operation under the same handicap as the other services, namely that the time-scale for working up was constantly varied or shortened. The intention of the Task Force Commanders was to be at Episkopi on Cyprus by D-10, but this could not be achieved. Difficulties were compounded by the congestion on the airfields in Cyprus as the strike force was assembled, and by the lack of accommodation. It was not until 1200 on 28 October that Air Marshal Barnett assumed operational control of all aircraft engaged in *Operation Musketeer*. He regarded the build up of the Air Task Force as 'piecemeal', and later declared that the operation 'was coloured and limited by political considerations from start to finish'.[21] By the time the operation was launched, the RAF had assembled a strong force of Venom FB4s, Hunter F5s, Canberra PR7s, Meteor NF13s and a wing of French F84s at Akrotiri; there were Canberra B2 bombers at airfields in Cyprus and Malta, and Hastings transport aircraft with French Noratlases and Dakotas at Tymbou in Cyprus. Valiant and Canberra B6 bombers, with their longer range, were based at Luqa and Hal Far on the island of Malta. The very size of this force presumed strong resistance from the Soviet equipped Egyptian Air Force.

Although a single high-level reconnaissance flight by a Canberra over the Egyptian coastline was carried out on 20 October, no further surveillance occurred until 28 October. Three sorties were flown on 29 October, thirteen the next day and eleven on 31 October. On one of these sorties, a Canberra was attacked and damaged by an Egyptian MiG-15 fighter. In addition to the coastline, these flights covered Egyptian airfields, military targets, blockships and Cairo radio station. Large quantities of intelligence photographs were produced, but there did not exist on Cyprus a Joint Services organisation to decide which material should have priority. Processing and interpretation personnel were lacking.[22] Consequently, photographic information often failed to reach the carrier squadrons before they launched their strikes.

The RAF bomber crews were ordered to be bombed up and at six hours readiness from 0700Z 30 October, but Allied bombing operations did not actually begin until 1615Z on 31 October when Royal Air Force Canberra and Valiant bombers attacked Egyptian airfields at Almaza, Inchas, Abu Suier and Kabrit, the raids continuing after dark. High level bombing, aimed at airfield runways, unfortunately included an attack, in error, on Cairo International Airport. On 1 November daylight ground attacks began in earnest with the aim of destroying the Egyptian Air Force on the ground. Royal Air Force targets were to the east of 32 degrees longitude. The land based Venoms, having to fly from their bases in Cyprus, were only able to spend some ten to fifteen minutes in the target area.[23]

British and French carrier borne aircraft with shorter distances to their targets, joined in the air offensive with strikes to the west, the Fleet Air Arm squadrons looking for aircraft on Egyptian airfields, particularly the Soviet built MiG and Ilyushin planes. The most profitable way for the subsonic Seahawks and Sea Venoms to deal with the potentially more dangerous MiGs was to catch them on the ground. It was for this reason that aircrew aboard the carriers had practised night flying. They would have to take off and form up in darkness in order to attack the Egyptian airfields at sunrise.

On 1 November, following the departure before sunrise of a reconnaissance Skyraider from *Eagle*, the 'troublesome' presence of the United States Sixth Fleet aircraft became evident for the first time. Two hours later the first ground attack machines were launched. Aboard the three carriers, the strike aircraft prepared to take off, last minute checks being made to each parked machine and its armament. Pilots were already in their cockpits as the ships turned into wind. The tannoy command of 'Stand clear of intakes and jet pipes. Start the jets.' was followed by the explosive sound of cartridge starters. The first strike aircraft moved forward, belly lights reflecting on the deck as they moved towards the catapult that would launch them on their first mission. *Eagle* dispatched her first strike to targets on the airfields, first at Inchas where Seahawks of 897 and 899 Squadron, and Sea Venoms of 892 and 893 squadrons destroyed and damaged a number of MiGs on the ground and damaged airfield installations. Lieutenant Philip Cardew, a young pilot in his first front line squadron, recalled flying as 'No 2' to Lt Cdr Bruce Clarke, 899 Squadron Commander on this strike. He flew one of eight Sea Hawks that took off from *Eagle* at 0520 local time. It was the first of four sorties he made that day that included a CAP, escorting Wyverns as they attacked Dekheila airfield and ending with a ground attack on the airfield at Cairo West. This last strike 'produced some intensive flak that we found rather frightening', especially as the squadron Commander called them in on the target three times.[24] Seven Wyverns of 830 Squadron bombed Dekheila (where the Russian built MiG and Ilyushin aircraft were being assembled), and they, too, attacked Cairo West. Escorted by Sea Hawks, they struck at the runways of Dekheila airfield with each aircraft carrying a 1000lb bomb. Two more strikes followed, making a total of 18 sorties without loss. Throughout the day, more attacks were made on the airfields, while Sea Hawks bombed the Egyptian blockship *Akka* to prevent it from being sunk in the buoyed channel. A particular target on this first day, *Akka* was initially observed moored in Lake Timsah, but later seen moving erratically to the southern end of the lake. The attack with bombs and rockets by a strike of twelve Sea Hawks of 897 and 899 Squadrons failed to sink the ship. Then later, when seen under tow, a further strike of eight Sea Hawks of 897 Squadron only, orbited while the strike leader sought an opportunity to sink her while she was clear of the channel. At a chosen moment two of the Sea Hawks were sent in, and the second aircraft, flown by Lieutenant Don Mills, made a direct hit aft. Believing that *Akka* would now sink, the remaining aircraft diverted to attack the airfield at Abu Sueir, not realising that the Egyptians would succeed in towing the damaged vessel into the main channel before she finally sank.

From *Bulwark*, 895 Squadron, formed rapidly out of training units and now fully worked up, became airborne in three divisions to strike at Dekheila, while at Cairo West the Fleet Air Arm strike arrived just as the last bombs were falling from RAF Valiant and Canberra attacks. *Albion* sent 8 Sea Hawks of 800 and 802 Squadrons, led by 4 Sea Venoms of 809 Squadron to attack Almaza, east of Cairo. They climbed to 15,000 feet and soon crossed the Nile Delta. Almaza appeared to starboard and the strike dived down onto the target, looking especially for MiGs on the ground. Some aircraft pulled out of their dives dangerously low, described by one pilot as 'a common error made by inexperienced pilots resulting from target fixation.' Other aircraft on the airfield were attacked and destroyed in a hail of cannon shells, before the formation headed for home at low level, pulling up at the coast and flying back to their carrier. As these first attacks went in, the strength of the resistance was unknown. The potential threat from the MiGs was real, but the quality of anti-aircraft gunfire would only be found out by experience. In the event, no enemy aircraft were encountered in the air, but many were destroyed on the ground. Two MiGs, seen by *Albion's* aircraft, had just taken off but did not interfere with the attack. The flak from the different targets was variously described as 'neither accurate nor effective', 'light and inaccurate' or 'almost non-existent'.[25] In the light of this experience, the initial tactic of 'one pass and away' could be adapted and targets once identified, could be attacked with more precision. On these initial strikes, the Sea Hawks only fired their 20mm cannon at the ground targets.

By the end of the day it was clear that much damage had been inflicted on the Egyptian Air Force, and no threat to the Task Force had materialised from the MiG fighters and Ilyushin bombers. Under instruction from Colonel Nasser to escape, a number of Egyptian aircraft had been flown to Syria, where they might subsequently be of use against further attacks by Israel. All the Royal Navy aircraft returned safely from their missions.

The possibility of E-boat attack kept the escorts alert. During the night of 1/2 November, the cruiser *Jamaica* picked up a suspect echo on radar and fired starshell. It was a false alarm, possibly caused by the destroyer *Duchess* straying from her sector.

While the Skyraiders flew barrier patrols, the second day of the campaign, 2 November, began as the first day had ended, with further attacks on Egyptian airfields. In a pre-dawn strike *Bulwark's* 895 Squadron Sea Hawk fighter-bombers attacked Bilbeis and Almaza, while in a similarly timed raid 802 Squadron from *Albion* also attacked airfields. *Eagle's* squadrons returned to Cairo West, Dekheila and Bilbeis in early morning raids. For a time, limitations were imposed upon strikes against Cairo West during a period when it was understood that American nationals were being evacuated along the adjacent road from Cairo to Alexandria. By noon, however, it was clear that the Egyptian Air Force had virtually ceased to exist. Attention therefore turned to Egyptian Army camps, particularly the Huckstep Camp east of Cairo, which was a known barracks and transport depot. The 897 Squadron diarist estimated that 85 tanks and some 500 vehicles were at the camp, but there may have been more. It was on this day that *Albion's* 800 Squadron ground attack aircraft fired rockets for the first time. Once it was known that there would be no opposition from the Egyptian Air Force, the Wyverns of 830 Squadron could operate further inland. They joined in the attacks on Huckstep Camp, each carrying one 1000lb bomb.[26]

By now the flak had become more intense, and the British carrier borne aircraft suffered their first casualty. A Sea Venom of 893 Squadron was hit by light flak during an attack on the airfield at Almaza and lost hydraulic power. The pilot, Lt Cdr John Willcox, was uninjured but it soon became clear to him that his observer, Flying Officer Bob Olding, one of two RAF navigators on loan to the squadron, was severely wounded. Lt Cdr Willcox made a perfect wheels up landing on *Eagle* at the second attempt, enabling Flying Officer Olding to be extricated from the plane and taken to *Eagle's* sickbay. Although flown by Skyraider to Cyprus, his wound became infected and his leg was amputated below the knee. Olding was awarded the DSC and in due course returned to a successful career in the RAF sporting an artificial leg. Other aircraft suffered damage.

Operations continued through a long day and it was not until 1810 that the last Skyraider barrier patrol landed on *Eagle*. Even then, one Skyraider crew was kept on standby throughout the night, just in case an attack by light coastal forces developed. At 2020 *Albion* detached from the carrier force and, in company with the New Zealand cruiser *Royalist*, headed north to rendezvous with the Underway Replenishment Group of 'Tide' class oilers and the RFA *Retainer*.[27] *Eagle* and *Bulwark* remained off the Egyptian coast to carry operations into the third day.

On 3 November, while *Bulwark's* aircraft attacked the hangars at Almaza, *Eagle's* Sea Venoms continued to attack airfields, but the Sea Hawks and Wyverns turned their attention to Gamil Bridge, an important target as it connected Port Said with the country west of the Nile Delta. In the course of these operations one 830 Squadron Wyvern aircraft was lost, when Lt Dennis MacCarthy's machine was hit by flak in a dive-bombing attack on the bridge. He turned towards the sea and managed to glide three miles out before ditching. He ejected safely. There followed a somewhat dramatic hour during which the CAP of Venoms was sent to cover him, and to silence the shore guns, which were taking pot shots at him. This they did.[28] MacCarthy was picked up by *Eagle's* Whirlwind helicopter after 75 minutes in the sea.

Despite near misses with 500lb and 1000lb bombs, the Gamil Bridge remained intact until late in the afternoon, when 899 Squadron mounted another strike with eight Sea Hawks, each carrying two 500lb bombs. They were escorted by Sea Hawks of 897 Squadron, whose task was to suppress any flak. The ground attack machines swept in low and were described as 'sticking their bombs into the bridge structure like darts and escaping before the 30 seconds delayed action fuses actuated the bombs'.[29] Success was evident in the gap left in the bridge at its western end. It had been intended that the bridge should be destroyed as soon after first light as possible, but it was not until 27 sorties had been flown that 'one third of the bridge from the West end' was reported as destroyed at 1620.[30]

On Sunday 4 November it was *Eagle's* turn to seek replenishment, leaving Captain Villiers of *Bulwark* in tactical command. Fuel was taken from the RFA *Tiderace* while RFA *Retainer* transferred ammunition. Being Sunday, a church service was held on the carrier's quarterdeck. During the afternoon, *Eagle's* helicopter lifted fresh bread from the carrier to *Duchess* and *Undine*.[31] In the meantime *Albion* and *Bulwark* continued operations. *Albion's* aircraft again attacked Almaza, before turning their attention to coastal defences as a softening up process prior to the imminent assault landings. Since rules of engagement laid down that every effort should be made to avoid civilian casualties, Fleet Air Arm pilots on armed reconnaissance were disconcerted to find that civilian refugees were clogging the roads from Cairo and making it impossible to strike at military traffic, unless in some way it became isolated from the refugees. From *Albion*, therefore, 802 Squadron flew against the flak defences at Almaza airfield, while 800 Squadron attacked the hangars with rockets. The Sea Hawks carried 500 lb bombs, which 'exploded with a bright flash raising tall columns of black smoke'. Reconnaissance later showed that most of the bombs had overshot the target because the pilots had let the speed of the aircraft get out of control. While Almaza continued to receive attention, strikes were also made against gun positions at Port Said and Port Fouad. Photographic reconnaissance missions were flown over Alexandria. It was noticeable that flak was now stronger and more accurate. Even though no aircraft were lost, Lt 'Nobby' Clarke of 802 Squadron had his cockpit canopy shattered by a 40mm shell bursting just above him; shrapnel entered the cockpit and made a hole in his helmet through to the inner lining. Just to show that hazards were not always from flak, Lt Jack Worth's aircraft suffered a bird strike. To add to the tally of the day's successes, Sea Venoms of 809 Squadron attacked three Motor Torpedo Boats heading towards Alexandria, damaging all three. Rocket firing aircraft from *Bulwark* then sank two of the three boats: the third was damaged, but was allowed to pick up survivors and make its way to base. *Bulwark's* squadrons, like those from *Albion*, dived on shore targets, especially gun positions. 895 Squadron, carrying rockets, aimed at two 6-inch gun positions at Port Said and destroyed a 6-pdr position at the end of the jetty.

Some anxiety must have been caused this day when, in the absence of *Eagle* for replenishment, *Albion* signalled to *Bulwark* 'Regret both catapults unserviceable'. However, in less than an hour and a half, repair to the starboard catapult was completed.

Monday, 5 November, was particularly significant, as this was the day that the airborne assault marked the first incursion of Allied land forces onto Egyptian territory. Codenamed *Operation Telescope*, it involved dropping both British and French parachute troops onto key locations. Orders had been written only 48 hours before the drop took place with the intention of putting forces on the ground in Egypt before a cease-fire could be ordered by the United Nations.[32] At 0820Z troops of the British 3 Parachute Battalion and 16 Parachute Brigade

Tactical HQ descended on Gamil Airfield, to the west of Port Said. Shortly afterwards 500 men of the 2 Regiment Parachutistes Coloniaux dropped close to the waterworks south of Port Said. Although flak was encountered and nine of the transport aircraft were hit, all returned to their base. In the meantime, despite strong resistance from light and heavy weapons, including Soviet self-propelled SU100 guns, the French soon secured their objectives, and by 0900 the airfield at Gamil was in British hands.

Unfortunately, when Vice Admiral Power was ordered to give priority support for *Operation Telescope*, he did not know what it was.[33] He was aware, however, that an aircraft had already gone to Akrotiri to collect important correspondence. This aircraft had landed aboard *Albion* after dark with material addressed to CTG 345.4. Vice Admiral Power instructed the Captain of *Albion* to open the envelopes, revealing four copies of the operational order. These were then delivered to *Eagle* and *Bulwark* by helicopter, the first time, it was believed, that such a flight had taken place after dark. One consequence of the advance by 24 hours of the first landing on Egyptian soil was that *Bulwark's* planned replenishment had to be postponed. In fact the ship remained operational for all six days of the campaign without pause. The French Carrier Task Unit could not be informed of the new orders as quickly as the British and had to be briefed on 'the inter-DO's circuit', a 'chat circuit' between Direction Officers. This apparent failure in communication meant that early air support for the paratroop landing had to be organised through inter-carrier briefing. All possible support must be given to the troops on the ground and air supremacy maintained. While British aircraft would cover the landing at Gamil, French aircraft would do the same for French troops engaged near the water filtration plant south of Port Said.[34]

Aircraft flew CAP patrols over the Fleet and some of them witnessed the arrival of a 'long straggling procession of transport aircraft' carrying the parachute troops. However, the carrier borne squadrons had other responsibilities that day in addition to supporting the troops on the ground. Before dawn *Eagle* launched eight Sea Venoms, four each from 892 and 893 Squadrons on intruder patrol which led to oil tanks to the west of Almaza airfield being set on fire as well as damage and destruction being inflicted on guns and aircraft. 899 Squadron Sea Hawks striking at the same airfields and damaging hangars followed them about an hour later. In recovering from their dive, the Sea Hawks passed very low over Cairo. Attacks were also carried out on Cairo West airfield. But once the paratroops had landed, the priority was to maintain Cabrank patrols. Resistance seemed slight and the Air Control Teams apologised for a lack of targets when so many aircraft were at their disposal. Attacks were however directed at the Coastguard Barracks, which had been turned into a defensive strong point. This large building was largely immune to rocket fire, so, acting on information from the ACT, Wyverns were launched carrying two 1000lb and one 500lb bombs each, fused to a 30 seconds delay. The knowledge gained in the earlier attack on Gamil Bridge was applied here. The strike was extremely accurate, though the Wyvern flown by the strike leader was lost to flak. Lt Cdr Bill Cowling, recognising that his aircraft had been hit, climbed to 1200 feet but had to throttle back. *Eagle* having acknowledged his Mayday call, Cowling ejected from his Wyvern some five or six miles from Port Said. As he landed in the sea, a Whirlwind helicopter, flown by Lt Cdr Jim Summerlee, was nearby transporting wounded soldiers back to the carrier. Cowling was quickly hauled aboard and, although he had to stand up for the journey, was soon back aboard *Eagle*.

At about 1500, news was received that the local Egyptian commander at Port Fuad wished to discuss surrender terms on behalf of the Governor and Military Commander. The message was passed to Brigadier M A H Butler DSO MC who was in command of the whole airborne assault and had landed at Gamil. By 1530 a Cease Fire was ordered and surrender terms agreed, only to be rescinded when referred to Cairo. Operations then resumed at 2030. The temporary cease-fire meant that offensive air operations also ceased for that period, but the patrolling aircraft were ever watchful. The three British carriers maintained a constant Cabrank of some 12 to 18 aircraft, while six Corsairs were available to the French ACT. Vice Admiral Power also reported this day that two MTBs were sighted off Port Said harbour by a CAP, which attacked and destroyed them. The diarists of 892 Squadron (*Eagle*) and 810 Squadron (*Bulwark*) reported the strike.

Two events that occurred aboard *Eagle* on 5 November demonstrated that flying to and from an aircraft carrier in darkness was in itself a hazardous undertaking. Two Sea Hawk pilots of 899 Squadron were descending down the mirror approach glide path, each unaware of the other's presence. When at last one pilot saw the other above him and almost in his cockpit, he waved off down the starboard side of the carrier. The other pilot, whose first night deck landing this was, pulled up sharply and in so doing, nearly stalled. Fortunately he recovered. The squadron diarist noted that this was one of several recent mirror circuit incidents, and the nearest to a fatality. The other event occurred when a 20mm shell 'cooked off' from a returning Sea Hawk, striking another Sea Hawk in the jet pipe where it was standing in the deck park in what was described as the congested area of 'Fly One'.[35] Although the aircraft hit by the shell was out of action for some time, nobody was hurt.

Tuesday, 6 November, finally saw the seaborne assault, when Royal Marine Commandos, supported by tanks, went ashore from landing craft. A reserve force was deployed shortly afterwards by helicopters from the carriers *Ocean* and *Theseus*. A CAP from *Albion*, having been launched in darkness, observed the fleet of landing craft carrying the assault troops as visibility improved. As the LCA were launched from their parent ships, they were seen to circle them 'like beetles on the water' before heading for the shore. Gun flashes out at sea were also visible. The air and naval fire plan to precede the assault on Port Said had been reduced in order to avoid civilian casualties and minimise damage to property. Indeed, air bombing had been prohibited. Nevertheless, the assault required close support from the carrier borne aircraft off Port Said. This included an air strike on the beaches ten minutes before the start of naval gunfire and a low level attack all along the beaches in the short interval between naval gunfire being halted and the leading troops reaching the shore.[36] For the squadrons the situation throughout the day must have seemed confused. The ships' flying programmes had to respond to the demands of the situation ashore. Cabrank patrols were maintained throughout, initiated by inter-carrier briefing. Strikes were sent out to attack such diverse targets as slit trenches and possible dug-in gun positions, self propelled guns, tanks, soft-skinned vehicles, and Egyptian troops possibly forming up for counter attacks against the assault forces.[37] When the aircraft arrived, the intended targets were not always visible. But it was now that the formation adopted by Vice Admiral Power was seen to be most effective, as each carrier could turn into wind to launch aircraft at immediate notice and without hindrance to the others. Even before the assault, naval aircraft engaged targets, their strikes being controlled by French Air Spot Teams and Air Alert Missions directed from HMS *Meon*, a converted River class frigate classified as a Landing Ship Headquarters (Small). Continuous support was therefore available. The Sea Venoms of 892 Squadron flew sixteen sorties in the day and claimed an Egyptian MTB, four or five Bren gun carriers and gun positions destroyed. Sea Hawks of 897 Squadron's first Cabrank were not given any targets by the British Air Control Teams (ACT) but were asked by the French to look at the Golf Course south of Port Said. Little was seen, but a possible dug-in gun position was attacked with rocket projectiles. From mid morning armed reconnaissance flights took place further south, many oil tankers and cargo vessels being observed at Suez, as well as small warships and patrol boats. An afternoon flight over Suez reported that there were in fact no MTBs at the base, nevertheless the MTB wharf and pier were attacked with rockets, setting the pier on fire and destroying two buildings. At El Quantara, an army camp was strafed and armoured fighting vehicles located in the vicinity were hit with rocket projectiles. In the early afternoon eight aircraft were flown off, and during this operation lost one of their number. In fact, during the day two aircraft were lost, a Sea Hawk of 800 Squadron from *Albion* and another Sea Hawk of 897 Squadron from *Eagle*. Lt John Stuart Jervis from 800 Squadron suffered an explosion in his engine, and ejected from his aircraft. He landed in the sea and was fortunate enough to be picked up by a boat launched from the Headquarters Ship *Meon*. Lt Donald Mills engaged some Egyptian tanks outside El Quantara, between Port Fouad and Ismailia. Having a problem with his gyro gun sight he was flying low when his aircraft was hit and a fire warning light came on. As he climbed, he called 'Mayday', jettisoned his hood and ejected. On landing he realised he was some forty miles behind enemy lines, though his No 2, Lt Gerry Maynard was circling overhead. Mills decided that he must put a distance between himself and his parachute, and after dark headed north towards Allied lines. He was gratified to see at first four French Corsairs from the carrier *La Fayette* arrive overhead, and then a division of Royal Navy Sea Hawks. The Corsairs had to depart, but the combined air cover prevented what appeared to be Israeli forces from approaching his position. Later he saw three divisions of aircraft above him, prepared to attack anything that threatened him. In good time, a Whirlwind helicopter of *Eagle's* ship's flight piloted by Lt Cdr Pete Bailey arrived and touched down, allowing Mills to climb aboard. Pausing only to refuel at the coast, the Whirlwind returned to *Eagle* with its relieved passenger.[38]

Some concern was expressed during the day over the use of Cabranks. 804 Squadron from *Bulwark* reported 'unsatisfactory conditions' when 'troops on the ground requested assistance repeatedly, but *Meon* refused it'.[39] The 899 Squadron diarist also mentioned the presence of vehicles at El Quantara, but reported that the pilots hesitated to shoot lest they harm civilians 'thus causing more international outcries'. Attempts to get through to the headquarters ship

Meon to obtain clearance 'took an age'. With the troops on the ground engaged in street fighting, targets were less easy to identify, especially with the directive to avoid civilian casualties. There was also the possibility that Allied troops might be subject to 'friendly fire', a tragedy that actually occurred when Wyvern aircraft from *Eagle* mistakenly attacked a command post of 45 Commando, Royal Marines, while they were halted in a built up area. Frustration was already evident as 'communication troubles, congested briefings and political inhibitions combined to make this a day on which the primary impression was one of wasted effort and air power'.[40] However, the last strike from *Eagle* was by six Sea Hawks of 899 Squadron, directed to attack Navy House, the old British Canal Zone Naval Headquarters. The Ground Liaison Officer knew this was a 'very tricky operation' because the leading Commandos were only some 80 yards away from the building. The attack with rockets and 20mm gunfire, well controlled from the ground, was so successful that it was called off by the ACT before completion.[41]

The regrettable 'friendly fire' incident occurred at 0845, and is fully described in the report of 3 Commando Royal Marines.[42] The sequence of events began when a destroyer supporting the landings reported that she was being fired on by an enemy gun. The destroyer, HMS *Decoy* (Captain P J Hill-Norton), returned fire but stopped when it became clear that there was a danger of hitting our own troops. When the gun fired again, *Decoy* requested the gun should be dealt with via the headquarters ship *Meon*, which had overall command of the Cabrank and allotted aircraft to the various ACT on the ground. The position was given with the gun being sited near a mosque with two minarets. The Joint Fire Support Committee (JFSC) ordered aircraft from a Cabrank to attack, calling down a division of three Wyverns of 830 Squadron. The mission leader was informed that British troops were 400 yards east of the target and was given the grid reference which he repeated correctly. He found an anti-tank gun near the mosque but thought it may be British. He was still told to carry on and attack. As a result, 45 Commando suffered 16 casualties, including the Commanding Officer, Lt Col N H Tailyour and the Intelligence Officer, Major Long. The pilot of the third aircraft said there were a number of troops on a nearby road (he gave the grid reference) and he dived on them firing 20mm cannon, thus causing the majority of casualties to the Commandos and two members of No 3 ACT. A Ground Liaison Officer, who had established an observation post on the roof of the police station on the west bank of the Canal, saw the attack. He was listening on the Ground Attack Common Channel and heard the report of a Wyvern pilot and the instructions from the JFSC in *Meon* instructing the pilot to attack. He tried to call the aircraft to abort the attack, but could not make contact. His opinion was that, as the target was inside the bomb line, the duty controller in *Meon* should have told the pilot to contact the nearest Air Control Team, namely No 3 ACT.[43] Vice-Admiral Power, in his report, having stated that the bombline was clearly defined and known to pilots, noted that the briefing was given to them on a 1:5000-scale map, but they were carrying maps of 1:100,000 scale. He also stated that attempts by the JFSC to pinpoint the target were confusing as there were several mosques as described with the beach to the north. He went on to say that the Wyvern section queried the target several times before picking out what they thought was the target. They were uncertain where our own troops were. Finally he emphasised that the strike was ordered without control from the ACT. No blame was attached to the Wyvern pilot. The report of 63 CBGL Section in HMS *Eagle* stated that the naval operation order specifically laid down that the 1:100,000 map would be used by all pilots when carrying out air strikes in support of requests from ground forces. The same scale map would be used by GLO (Ground Liaison Officers) and CBGLOs in their briefing and by FAO (Forward Air Controllers) in controlling air to ground attacks. This strike was briefed by a JFSC controller using a 1:5000 scale map. It is likely that the Wyvern pilots thought an Air Control Team near the intended target was briefing them.

At 2359 on 6 November a cease-fire came into operation. General Keightley received orders from London at 1700Z that United Nations Forces would take over and that the leading Allied troops would halt at midnight. General Stockwell ordered his troops to get as far south as possible down the Suez Canal, and by the time of the cease fire they had reached El Cap, about 23 miles south of Port Said. This meant that thereafter, Cabrank sorties ceased, though CAP were to be maintained. Significantly, on this day *Eagle's* port catapult, having sustained all launches from the ship during the campaign, was declared unserviceable. 621 launches were made from this one catapult during *Operation Musketeer*, most of them loaded and armed jet aircraft. No further launches of jet aircraft could take place, therefore Vice Admiral Power reported that *Eagle* would be unserviceable as a carrier for 8 to 10 days. He stated that he intended to remain on board, the more effectively to maintain control and administer the carrier force in giving support to the assault on Port Said.[44] The next day, however, the cease-fire having come into operation, he transferred his flag to *Bulwark*, *Eagle* being forced to return to Malta for catapult repairs. Before leaving the area, *Eagle* approached to within about four miles of Port Said to transfer to *Theseus* those casualties that had been brought on board during operations. Midshipman Howard noted in his journal:

> From about six miles out, dozens of merchant ships were anchored in the swept channel approaching the canal waiting to go inshore and unload their cargoes of stores, lorries and ammunition. There were large numbers of warships there also, including the French battleship *Jean Bart*, the cruisers *Georges Leygues* and *De Grasse* and the British cruisers *Jamaica* and *Ceylon*. Not very much could be seen of Port Said itself except a forest of masts in the harbour and the outline of houses, overshadowed by a pall of smoke from an oil fire to the south of the town.[45]

Two days later *Eagle* arrived at Malta.

The French Carrier Task Force.

The French carriers *Arromanches* and *La Fayette*, commanded by Contre Admiral Yves Caron as Flag Officer (Air) Mediterranean, came under the overall command of Vice Admiral Power on the morning of 31 October. Operating instructions had already been issued to them, giving FOAC's intentions as soon as *Operation Musketeer* was ordered. It had already been agreed that the French force should operate within about 15 miles of the British force, and that the French Avengers would be responsible for all daylight anti-submarine patrols, a responsibility which Vice Admiral Power admitted, 'must have been extremely boring'. At the same time they must be ready to strike at any enemy surface ships detected during the day. French naval aircraft were also employed on shipping reconnaissance in an area that was confused by the presence of British, French, American, neutral and enemy shipping.

On 1 November, French bomb carrying Corsairs damaged the Egyptian frigate *Tariq* (ex-HMS *Whimbrel*) and *Al-Nasr*, an ex-Soviet Skory class destroyer, though both ships sailed on to Alexandria. On 2 November two Corsairs from *La Fayette* attacked what they thought was an Egyptian MTB. It was in fact the French submarine *La Creole*, which dived as soon as it became clear that their fellow countrymen were intent upon their destruction. Although the Corsairs claimed to have sunk the 'MTB', the submarine suffered no damage. It was also on 2 November that a Corsair was lost over the side of *La Fayette*. On the following day French aircraft turned their attention to targets on land and bombed Cecelia airfield. Once air superiority was assured Corsairs were free to attack inland targets, notably Cairo Almaza airfield, cratering the runways and damaging hangars. It was during this attack that a Corsair Squadron Commander, Lt de V Lancrenon, flying from *Arromanches*, was shot down by Egyptian anti-aircraft fire and killed. Like the British, the French were forced to observe the requirement to avoid civilian casualties and had to cease armed reconnaissance of the Tel el Kebir - Ismailia road.

The situation changed when the carriers were required to support the paratroop landings on 5 November. But the day began with two Avengers attacking Egyptian surface vessels and narrowly avoiding contact with fighters from the US Sixth Fleet. To support the paratroops, two new operating areas were approved, one being used by the French and the other by the British. While the Fleet Air Arm aircraft supported the landing at Gamil airfield, the French carrier borne Corsairs supported the French airborne landing south of Port Fouad. Six French Corsairs were constantly available to attack targets of opportunity in response to requests from the French ACT. French troops occupied Port Fouad during the night 5th/6th November, just prior to the sea borne landings. Throughout 6 November, Corsairs from *Arromanches* and *La Fayette* flew French Air Alert Missions under the control of HMS *Meon*. They gave continuous support to the assault troops by attacking Egyptian positions and fuel and ammunition dumps. One Corsair was lost. When Lt Mills ejected over enemy territory, six Corsairs joined Sea Hawks and Sea Venoms in providing a rescue CAP.

Throughout the campaign, the French were somewhat handicapped by the obsolete Corsairs and Avengers with which they were equipped. It was recognised that they would be particularly vulnerable to Egyptian MiGs until the Egyptian Air Force had been eliminated as a fighting force. Once this was achieved, however, French Corsairs in particular flew sorties inland, attacking military targets and supporting first the parachute drops and later the French contingent in the sea assault. They took part also in cab rank patrols and the Avengers maintained their anti-submarine patrols. French naval aircraft had their share of interference from the US Sixth Feet, but managed to avoid any 'incident' with US Navy fighters. At the end of the operation, Vice Admiral Power was able to report, however, that 'the Corsair proved, with its mixed armament load of bombs and rockets, strikingly effective'.[46]

Before the campaign began, two Allied submarines, the French *La Creole* and the HM Submarine *Tudor*, had sailed from Malta on 28 October to take up their separate Search and Rescue (SAR) positions off the Egyptian coast should any Allied aircraft be forced to ditch in the sea. Lt Cdr W G Edwards commanded *Tudor*. Being tall, dark and formidable in appearance, he was known as 'The Black Mamba', or 'Sluggy' due to earlier boxing skills in the Royal Navy. Before sailing, the ship's company painted over the brightwork, dismantled the indicator buoys, and prepared the torpedo warheads. By 0700 on 1 November *La Creole* was in her allocated position, described as S2. *Tudor*, having adopted silent routine and shut off for depth charging,[47] assumed it had reached its position S1, but an apparently reliable star sight some two hours later put the boat 23 miles east of S1 and therefore well outside its patrol zone. It seems likely that, because the submarine was running radio silent, the deck clock could not be checked, and the boat's correct position was uncertain. With his submarine's 'snort' raised, Lt Cdr Edwards headed westwards at maximum speed. Whilst proceeding, a message was received of a reported aircraft ditching 7 miles from the Port Said light.[48]

Vice Admiral Power, aboard HMS *Eagle*, found himself unable to contact *Tudor* when the aircraft went down. He signalled to the Commander of the 1st Submarine Flotilla (SM1) that, '*Tudor* may not be aware there is very little air threat, but it is essential that she can receive signals from *Eagle* day and night if she is to be able to perform her function'. He requested that *Tudor* be informed accordingly, at the same time complaining that he had not been able to contact *La Creole* either when he wanted her.[49]

In fact, *Tudor*'s 'fix' was in error and the boat was heading away from the correct position towards *La Creole*. The French submarine gained contact but could not be certain that this was a friendly submarine. It was unlikely to be Egyptian, but it could be a Russian boat. Therefore it began to manoeuvre into a firing position. On contacting the Task Force Commander, *La Creole* was ordered to fire only in self-defence since the other boat could be *Tudor*.[50] On being challenged, *Tudor* replied. It was also said that *La Creole* recognised the snort mast as being that of the British 'T' class. In the early afternoon, with the danger of a disastrous attack by one Allied submarines upon another having been averted, *Tudor* was able to obtain a correct fix and so returned to S1.

In fairness to *Tudor*, submarine navigation was largely as in World War 2, while communication with submarines, via the Rugby radio masts and home made whip H/F aerials, was often poor.[51] There was also an understandable reluctance on the part of a submarine to reveal its presence.

No further events occurred before the cease-fire on 6 November and at 1406 7 November the two boats were ordered to return to Malta. The two submarines had not been required to rescue any aircrew from the sea. Indeed, so uneventful was the patrol that *Tudor*'s First Lieutenant spent much of his time knitting a christening shawl for his expected first child, a garment that smells of Diesel to this day![52]

The aircraft carriers and their squadrons could hardly have done more. The ships' speed and mobility demonstrated the flexibility of a carrier force. When high level bombing proved ineffective and shore based RAF fighters had to operate at the limit of their endurance, the Fleet Air Arm could provide half the initial strike force and practically all the close support for the airborne and sea assaults. Before the short campaign began it was uncertain whether the Egyptian Air Force would mount serious opposition, not only to Allied attacks, but also to the presence of the carriers themselves. The threat did not materialise, partly because of the highly successful early ground attacks by Fleet Air Arm aircraft, which destroyed or damaged many Egyptian machines. The inferior performance of the Allied aircraft did not matter, therefore, on this occasion, but being lucky once does not hide the need for aircrew to be wholly confident that their equipment is able to meet the demands likely to be made upon it. As Air Marshal Sir Denis Barnett put it in his report on *Operation Musketeer*:

> ...there is no doubt that if we had been up against an enemy, with even a modicum of fighting qualities, with the modern aircraft and equipment the Egyptians had, the situation would have been different.[53]

Of the three British carriers, only *Eagle* was fully prepared when the operation against Egypt loomed. Both *Albion* and *Bulwark* had to be brought forward hurriedly, and it is greatly to the credit of their ship's companies and air groups that they were worked up when the operation actually began. But perhaps the most serious shortcoming was the inability of the hydraulic catapult fitted to the carriers to sustain heavy use in launching jet aircraft. *Eagle* began the operation without one of her two catapults and when the other broke down at the end of the campaign, the ship was forced to withdraw completely. *Albion* too had trouble with her catapults. *Bulwark* reported that her port catapult started to fail on 4 November. Later, fortunately after *Operation Musketeer* was over, but not before the final withdrawal of Allied forces from Egypt in December, her starboard catapult acceleration rope failed on 29 November.[54] Great credit must be given to the carrier force for its ability to sustain operations of considerable intensity. The three British carriers benefited from their angled decks and from the mirror landing sights. They achieved a high sortie rate, which in itself suggests very satisfactory serviceability, thorough training, effective operational techniques and sound equipment. In consequence, the Fleet Air Arm did not suffer the high attrition rate that it had to endure during World War II.

There is evidence of some failures in communication and intelligence. The Ground Liaison Section aboard *Eagle* found that the naval picture ' was kept up to date entirely by tactical photographic and armed reconnaissance by carrier aircraft'. Many reports, for example those concerning the possible presence of enemy submarines, and the disposition of the Egyptian army were vague. Indeed 'up to the landing, information on the military situation was mainly derived from the BBC'. After the cease-fire scarcely any information was passed from the Headquarters of the British 2nd Corps. To take a specific case, photographic cover of the blockship *Akka*, located 3.5 cables south of the Canal Company workshop at Lake Timsah would have enabled more precise planning to determine the method of attack, direction and number of aircraft required to sink the ship out of the shipping lanes. Then again, aircraft sent to attack the Gamil

Bridge had no idea of its construction, its eventual destruction being due to photographs taken by attacking aircraft. The 'friendly fire' episode demonstrated the importance of those controlling air to ground strikes having maps of the same scale as the pilots carrying out the air strikes.[55] Vice Admiral Power's Summary of Operations during *Operation Musketeer* concluded:

> These operations in which the Carrier Squadron were honoured to take a leading part have proved that the training of the aircrew, the aircraft and the carriers themselves are capable of achieving all and more than could be asked of them in a limited war of this description.[56]

The significance of Vice Admiral Power's commendation is put into a new perspective by a note from the First Sea Lord, Admiral Earl Mountbatten of Burma, at the end of the file.

> Vice Admiral Power had been notorious in the Navy for writing down the quality of service of officers, and had frequently been accused of expecting an unattainably high standard. When he was my Chief of Staff I used to have to amend his reports of my staff officers since I had a higher opinion of them than he had expressed.
> I could therefore scarcely believe my eyes when I read this paean of praise, but then no carrier force in history that I have heard of has finished a week's continuous operating at maximum rate with a serviceability of 99% and I doubt if any other Navy or Air Force could equal this...[57]

Admiral Earl Mountbatten's reference to 'continuous operating at maximum rate' recognised the achievement of ships' companies, aircrew and maintenance crews. The pilots, however, were becoming fatigued, having carried out a large number of operational sorties over six days. One pilot recalled that as he approached the deck of the carrier after his last sortie on 6 November, his Seahawk landed with the usual heavy impact, but there was no deceleration and he shot off the front of the flight deck to try again. He was informed that he had failed to lower his arrester hook, normally part of the cockpit check as he flew in the circuit before landing. Tiredness was the cause and this suggests that some aircrew and probably maintenance crews were reaching the limit of endurance in operations of such intensity. Although hostilities ceased at midnight on 6 November, the carriers still had a role to fulfil in providing cover for British and French forces on the ground as well as the concentration of shipping present at Port Said. Although the three carriers had to withdraw in turn for replenishment at sea or sail to Malta for essential maintenance, they would continue to provide air cover until the final withdrawal of British and French forces in December.

Chapter 4

Ocean and Theseus: The Helicopter Assault

The morning of 6 November 1956 found the carriers *Ocean* (Captain I W T Beloe DSC RN) and *Theseus* (Captain E F Pizey DSO RN), designated TG 345.9, anchored off Port Said and poised to begin an operation that would make history. In command of the squadron was Rear Admiral G B Sayer CB DSO, flying his flag in *Ocean*. Rear Admiral Sayer had considerable wartime experience. He commanded the destroyer *Cleveland* in support of the raid on Saint Nazaire in March 1942. Later he was involved in the preparatory stages of *Operation Torch*, the landings in North Africa. Then after the end of the war against Germany, he served as Captain of Naval Assault Force 'A', engaged in *Operation Zipper*, the intended landing in Malaya in 1945. The two ships of his Home Fleet Training Squadron, aircraft carriers of the 'Colossus' class were about to take on a new role. They were not new ships, *Ocean* having been completed in the summer of 1945 and *Theseus* early the following year. They displaced some 18,000 tons when fully loaded. Built to mercantile standards, they were lightly armoured and armed, their major asset being a flight deck 690 feet long and 80 ft wide. Both ships had operated fixed wing aircraft during the Korean War, but their most recent commission had been as the Home Fleet Training Squadron. In this role, they resembled fleet carriers in outward appearance only. They had not been converted to angled deck carriers. Instead, two hangars became home for hundreds of men under training, a third was converted into classrooms and on the flight deck, instead of Fireflies and Sea Furies, lay a number of boats. While it was still possible to embark helicopters, they would have to operate from the limited space that remained on the flight deck, only being stowed below if there was a danger that the aircraft would be damaged in severe weather. Both *Ocean* and *Theseus* had carried a flight each of 845 Squadron, with their Whirlwind helicopters operating in an anti-submarine role. During *Exercise Fairwind* in July 1956, thickening fog had limited the helicopters to a few sorties, but it had been shown that their presence did not upset the ships' normal routine.[1]

The idea of using a converted aircraft carrier for Combined Operations was not new. As early as 1950, a paper had been produced at combined Operations Headquarters, wherein it was suggested that the hulls of three 15,700-ton

'Leviathan' class carriers might be fitted out to carry LCA.[2] Their speed would be a great asset, but even then it was recognised that such large ships would be vulnerable in an opposed landing unless air superiority could be assured, either by shore-based aircraft or, as in *Operation Musketeer*, by carrier-borne fixed wing aircraft.

The potential value of helicopters in amphibious warfare, or 'vertical envelopment', was already understood. In the United States Navy, the former escort carrier *Thetis Bay* was converted into an Assault Helicopter Aircraft Carrier, capable of carrying assault troops and 15 helicopters.[3] The ship was commissioned in her new role on 20 July 1956, having been designated CVHAA1. The British had good intentions, but not for the first or last time, were hampered by limited financial resources and political commitment. Despite support from Earl Mountbatten, with his considerable experience of combined operations, priority in the use of Royal Navy helicopters was given to Anti-submarine Warfare (ASW) and Air Sea Rescue (ASR) roles. A paper presented by Amphibious Warfare HQ in July 1955 foresaw the helicopter carrier as the troop carrier of the future and hoped that an existing helicopter squadron might add amphibious training to its tasks. Limited trials were carried out in May 1955 when, in *Exercise Runaground*, two Whirlwind and four Dragonfly aircraft of 705 Helicopter Training Squadron lifted men from two platoons of 42 Royal Marine Commando in an exhibition training exercise that involved landings on Brown Down Range near Gosport. In command of 705 Squadron at the time was Lieutenant Commander J C Jacob RN who subsequently led 845 Squadron in *Operation Musketeer* after it had been rapidly converted from its anti-submarine role.[4]

With the deterioration in the political situation in the Middle East, plans were drawn up for *Operation Musketeer*. It was suggested in late August that seizing the southern exits to Port Said early in an assault could be done by helicopter-borne troops. These aircraft could also be used for the evacuation of casualties from the beachhead and to meet any possible submarine threat arising from the purchase of Polish submarines by the Egyptian Navy.[5] A change of plan on 25 October cancelled the use of a helicopter force to attack bridges because to land a number of helicopters close to a defended area was an untried method. Furthermore, more helicopters would be needed than were available to lift a force large enough to seize and hold the objective. Uncertainty continued to surround the use of helicopters in the assault. At first it was thought that they might be used to land troops on the golf course when that area had been cleared. Paratroops might, however, render this unnecessary. Next, 45 Royal Marines Commando, aboard the two carriers, was given the role of a floating reserve available at the discretion of the Task Force Commanders. Finally, but not until 3 November was approval given for the airborne Commandos to land by helicopter, once the beachhead was in Allied hands. Options for this landing were the golf course, landing areas near the beaches, or near the de Lesseps statue.[6]

Once the helicopter assault had taken place, and the Royal Marine Commandos were ashore, then *Ocean* and *Theseus* could receive casualties. This meant that certain alterations had to be made to the ships before they left the United Kingdom. The after hangars were converted into auxiliary operating theatres and wards, while modifications were made to the mess decks and sick bay flat. At the same time B hangars were cleared for the operation of helicopters and the after fuel systems re-activated.

The helicopters destined to carry out the assault landing in Egypt were in two squadrons, but drawn from all three services. 845 Squadron Fleet Air Arm, commanded by Lt Cdr J C Jacob RN was made up of eight Whirlwind HAS22, built in the United States, and two Whirlwind HAR3 machines. The other squadron, known as the JHU (Joint Helicopter Unit), was initially an experimental formation (JEHU), composed of six Whirlwind HAR2 and six Army Sycamore 14 aircraft. In command was Lt Col F F T Scott, with Squadron Leader D C L Kearns AFC RAF as his deputy.

845 Squadron had reformed in November 1955 as an anti-submarine squadron being largely based at Eglinton, Northern Ireland. In April it took part in Joint Anti-Submarine School exercises, after which its aircraft were deployed separately in *Ocean* and *Theseus* for overseas visits. The Squadron's role changed on 22 September 1956 when it transferred to Lee-on-Solent for troop lift exercises. It was not until 29 September that seven helicopters of the squadron embarked in *Ocean* at Devonport with the task of preparing to work up with the Royal Marine Commandos. The eighth aircraft had a supercharger failure and had to remain at Lee-on-Solent for an engine change.[7] On 1 October the ship moved into Plymouth Sound and the first deck landings were practised with the ship at anchor. Two days later *Ocean* sailed for Spithead where mass take off and landing practices worked up the deck handling parties. Ten aircraft were on board by 6 October, and then exercises began in company with *Theseus*. Briefly, it seemed likely that *Ocean* would revert to her training role, so 845 Squadron transferred to *Theseus* while the Joint Helicopter Unit returned to Middle Wallop. The crisis deepened almost at once, so that, after loading stores and week end leave, *Theseus* sailed for the Mediterranean on 22 October with 400 troops on board as well as the helicopter squadron. Having reached Malta, eight aircraft disembarked to Hal Far and troop lifting familiarisation exercises were carried out with the Commandos. When hostilities broke out between Egypt and Israel, aircraft and ground crew immediately returned to the ship. Troops and Royal Marines were also embarked.

The Joint Helicopter Unit had been ordered to prepare for overseas service as early as 25 August 1956. The intention then was that the squadron would act as a close support and transport squadron under Royal Air Force control. Nevertheless, preplanning for a Commando assault was also carried out. The squadron was brought up to full war strength in both personnel and equipment, with enough spares to operate for 30 days. Initial practice was carried out at Middle Wallop with a carrier deck being marked out on the ground with tape. When its helicopters embarked on *Theseus* on 1 October, equipment included two petrol bowsers for refuelling trials. There followed twelve days of deck handling, deck landing, formation flying and mass flying with 845 Squadron. The squadron, made up of Army and Royal Air Force personnel, many of whom were aboard an aircraft carrier for the first time, recognised the value of integrating the JHU ground crews with sailors of the ship's air division to produce an effective team. It was also found that the tempo was much faster on board, where delay in launching aircraft could threaten the safety of the ship.

Authorisation was given for the conversion of both *Ocean* and *Theseus* to operational helicopter carriers on 25 September 1956, although extra equipment, structural alterations and additional personnel were required, the ships must still be able to carry out their previous trooping role at short notice. Both ships must have identical facilities so that different types of helicopter could be operated from each ship. With the conversion completed, mass helicopter trials took place between 29 September and 12 October.[8] The aim was to find the most effective means of operating a large number of helicopters in order to land 450 Commandos on an objective some 15 miles from the ships. Any problems arising from the operation of 22 helicopters from two ships in company would be met and resolved. Exercises began with independent landings, *Ocean* being in Plymouth Sound and *Theseus* in the Spithead area. *Ocean* sailed for Spithead on 3 October so that the ships could operate their aircraft together. Combined flying exercises actually began on 9 October and continued for four days. Unfortunately a full rehearsal of an assault landing at RNAS Ford, carried out in the presence of senior officers including the CinC Portsmouth, was severely restricted by poor visibility, but Rear Admiral Sayer remained convinced that the carriers and their squadrons were capable of performing their task. He recorded that 845 Squadron had made 402 trouble free landings and the JHU had made 607 such landings during the two weeks they were embarked. Remarkably, throughout the trial period, it was possible to get 21 aircraft airborne. Unserviceability, 'usually the bugbear of trials involving aircraft, was practically unknown'.[9] Rear Admiral Sayer went further and recommended that the possibility be considered of operating twenty-two helicopters from a single Light Fleet Carrier.[10] After inspection by senior officers, including Admiral Sir George Creasy on 12 October, 845 Squadron transferred from *Ocean* to *Theseus* while *Ocean* prepared to receive the JHU helicopters. On 27 October *Ocean* sailed for Malta, arriving on the last day of the month, and began immediately to carry out familiarisation flights with troops of 45 Royal Marines Commando wearing full battle equipment. It was also necessary to solve problems caused by awkward loads, notably the 106mm anti-tank rifle.

With different aircraft aboard each carrier, separate arrangements had to be made for ranging them on deck. *Ocean* spotted her ten Whirlwinds on numbered marks 70 feet apart, while *Theseus* spotted her six Whirlwinds on numbered marks, three forward of the island and three aft. The six Sycamores were ranged abreast the island and so placed that they could be moved rapidly to spots vacated by the Whirlwinds. One Sycamore would remain abreast the island.

The ships carried out night ranging under 'darken ship', established conditions under which rotors could be started and stopped, practised formation flying, refuelling and the mustering and emplaning the troops. Then, on 30 October, 845 Squadron Record Book stated that, 'Israel has invaded Egypt and Britain is taking immediate steps to counter the threat to the Suez Canal'. The threat of war between Britain, France and Egypt dramatically increased. The first impact on the squadron was the recall, from the Task Force, by the Canadian government, of Lieutenant Muncaster RCN, demonstrating the firm belief in much of the Commonwealth that any British and French action, without the support of the United Nations, was unacceptable.

The Assault.

The Joint Operation Order No 2, issued by Rear Admiral Sayer to the two squadrons, laid down detailed orders on the procedure for the execution of the mission to land 45 Commando in the beachhead area at Port Said when ordered by the force commander.[11]

On 3 November, approval was given for 45 Commando to be landed by helicopter once the beachhead had been secured. Both carriers therefore sailed from Malta, without escort, *Theseus* taking station 5 cables astern of *Ocean*. On board were the assault troops of 45 Royal Marine Commando and the men of No 215 Wing RAF, whose task would be to operate Gamil airfield once it had been captured. With last minute preparations completed, including deck landing trials and Bofors firing practice, vehicles were struck below and the helicopters ranged on the deck. With a possible submarine threat, *Theseus'* log noted that the ship commenced zigzagging early in the morning of 5 November, by which time the sea assault convoy was visible ahead of the carriers. Because of the innovative nature of the operation, careful consideration was given to the most effective method of ferrying the troops ashore. It was known that there were not enough helicopters available to land the whole force in one lift. The aircraft could therefore either land in waves or in a stream. In waves the helicopters would orbit, then fly in one formation to the Landing Zone (LZ) and land simultaneously or in divisions. To operate in a stream, the aircraft would proceed to and from the LZ individually, a method that would deliver more personnel and stores in a given time, but would land the troops in very small numbers. In the operation itself, both methods were used as seemed appropriate. A strict timetable was laid down, allowing 45 seconds to emplane, 15 seconds to deplane troops only, 27 seconds to deplane troops and stores. The run in to the LZ, seven miles distant should take 6 minutes. On return to the carrier, 15 minutes was allowed for turn round without refuelling and 21 minutes if refuelling was required.

There were of course variations in the load capacity of the different helicopters. 845 Squadron aircraft had been stripped of their anti-submarine sonar equipment, enabling the Whirlwind Mk 22 aircraft to carry a useful load of 1320 lbs or seven fully equipped marines while the Whirlwind Mk 3 could lift 1100 lbs or six men. The Joint Helicopter Unit Whirlwind Mk 2 could also lift six men, but the Sycamores could only manage 660 lbs or three fully equipped troops. The Sycamore was recognised as being unsuitable for carrier operations. Lt Col Scott reported a number of limitations. The wooden rotor blades were too flexible and susceptible to careless handling, the tail rotor blades swept low and were a hazard to personnel on deck. Doors had to be removed for rapid emplaning when troops were carried and replaced for stores and casualties. The tail skid fouled deck obstructions. It may have been effective in its original role of search and rescue, liaison etc, but it was unsatisfactory as a troop carrier and less than ideal as an aircraft carrier borne helicopter. The three Marines on board had to sit on the floor, the man in the middle holding his two companions whose legs dangled over the side. The two men could each carry a shell for the 106mm anti-tank guns, a projectile three feet long. The man in the middle could have six mortar bombs. Although they lacked handholds, at least the six Marines carried by the Whirlwinds were held within the helicopter. Despite its limited capacity, the Sycamore met the demands of *Operation Musketeer*.

As the two helicopter carriers steamed towards the Eastern Mediterranean, 845 Squadron carried out final flying practice, while the aircrews were given small arms training, issued with khaki clothing and emergency packs. On 5 November, the day on which paratroops landed in the Port Said area, the final briefing was held. Action would come the next day, with both *Ocean* and *Theseus* prepared for the tasks assigned to them, namely the landing of the Royal Marine Commando by 22 helicopters, the evacuation of casualties and any subsequent transport duties. This would be followed by the transport of troops, vehicles and stores to Port Said as part of the follow up operation. Each ship was prepared to receive and care for up to 75 casualties.[12]

In preparation for the landing, vehicles were struck down on the evening of 5 November and the helicopters ranged on deck. Early in the morning of 6 November, in accordance with Joint Operations Order No 2, *Ocean* and *Theseus* dropped anchor 5 cables apart in the swept channel some 8 miles off Port Said. The weather was fine and the sea smooth, and it was possible to observe the distant sea landings from the carriers. Aboard *Ocean*, as the ship entered waters that could be mined, cabins and messes were secured for battle, with hammocks and beds stowed below the hangar deck. On entering the swept channel off Port Said, hands were called to Action Stations. Commandos and aircrew were given set times for breakfast, while tea and sandwiches were made available in the Main Galley.

Commander S H Suthers, Commander (Air) in *Ocean*, posted orders for L Day, 6 November. At 0400 Action Stations were sounded for all, except aircrew. Other ranks of the JHU were called and sent to breakfast. Aircrew were shaken at 0445 and went to breakfast at 0500. At 0515, 45 Royal Marines Commando mustered in 'A' hangar, and at the same time the Sycamore helicopter rotor blades were spread. At 0545, by which time it was half-light, aircrew mustered in the Pilots' Briefing Room and came to 15 minutes notice for take off. By then the first 'sticks' of Commandos were on the flight deck. Marshals guided the Royal Marines to their helicopters, while the second wave in turn mustered in the hangar. Dawn was at 0615. Finally, at 0645, designated 'H' hour, aircraft were manned and at 10 minutes notice for take off.[13] The squadrons were at short notice for flying, but it was not until some 50 minutes after the sea landings began that orders were received to ferry the Royal Marine Commandos ashore. They would take off in divisions and fly to the landing zone in divisional sub groups at three-minute intervals. The first 845 Squadron helicopter to lift off from *Theseus* was piloted by the Senior Pilot, Lt Cdr R R Crayton RN with Capt J F B Shaw RASC, who had transferred from the JHU, as his co-pilot. They landed on board *Ocean* to pick up the Marine Commando Command Team consisting of five men led by their commander, Lt Col Norman Tailyour. Their task was to find a suitable landing ground for the full helicopter landing. Crayton had actually dropped the troops on a football field when, observing that they had come under fire, he immediately landed again to lift them off. Although hit 22 times, the Whirlwind flew on to the de Lesseps Landing Zone and successfully put down the Command Team. Lt Cdr Crayton returned to the carrier, still apparently unaware that his aircraft was damaged. He could apparently hear nothing with his helmet on. In the light of the opposition at the football field, an immediate decision was made to land the main force near the de Lesseps statue.

Lt Col Scott, to his regret, was unable to lead the Joint Helicopter Unit on the operation, as he was required by Rear Admiral Sayer to remain with him on *Ocean*'s bridge. The Sycamore Flight Commander aboard *Ocean* was Major F Graham Bell, who had served in the Fleet Air Arm during and after the Second World War. He joined the RNVR in 1941 and transferred to a Short Service Commission in 1945 until 1949. He later flew with the RASC before joining the JHU. When *Ocean* arrived in the Grand Harbour at Malta, he recalled his last posting there eight years before in the carrier *Triumph*. Now he stood on the flight deck of *Ocean* with the 2nd in command of the JHU, Sqdn Ldr D C L Kearns SFC, waiting to be told where to land the troops. He has described how, when Lt Col Scott informed them that they were to land in De Lesseps Square, they only knew of its location because his mother had once sent him a postcard, which had referred to a magnificent statue of Ferdinand de Lesseps seen as you enter the Suez Canal. The lack of appropriate maps seems to have been a feature of the campaign, all the more surprising when one remembers that British forces had only left Egypt a few months previously, after many years of occupation

The main force of 21 helicopters flew in four waves at intervals of about two minutes. Six Whirlwinds of the JHU led the way, followed by 5 Whirlwinds of 845 Squadron. Then came the six Sycamores of the JHU followed by four Whirlwinds of 845 Squadron. The area around the de Lesseps statue was sandy and just large enough for six aircraft in tight formation. Six Whirlwinds from *Theseus* were followed by 5 Whirlwinds from *Ocean* with successive groups following in a similar manner until a less rigid procedure was adopted for later stores and personnel. Of the initial assault, Graham Bell recalled:

> We flew in low at 70 knots, and because the landing area was confined and partly obscured by smoke blowing across from the town, we had to keep close to the Whirlwinds in front in order to give a rapid back up, but not too close so that we would have to come to the hover while they moved away.[14]

Of 845 Squadron, the Record Book states:

> Within about two hours all Commandos were ashore without incident. Four aircraft were sent to the main carrier force to bring back casualties brought off the previous day and on the return flight the Whirlwind piloted by Lt Morgan was forced to ditch. His two (French) casualties were both saved, one by the accompanying Whirlwind of Lt Speller, and the other by Lt Cooper, flying from the ship. For the remainder of the day the squadron stood by for casualty evacuation.

Lt Morgan was returning from a casualty evacuation mission to the Carrier Task Group, 30 miles out to sea. A similar mishap nearly occurred when Flight Lieutenant Stuart, on loan from the JHU and carrying wounded men, landed on deck just as he ran out of fuel. The only setback to the Sycamore Flight was an engine failure when the machine piloted by Captain J B Shaw RASC lifted off on its second flight. The helicopter was quickly pushed out of the way and operations continued. After landing their troops, the helicopters returned to the ship, landed on and were reloaded in just one or two minutes. It was only after the second sortie that the aircraft were refuelled, loading and refuelling taking three to four minutes for each wave of six aircraft. When the Commando lift was completed, *Ocean's* Royal Marines Detachment was ferried to join the forces already ashore and the advance party of 215 Wing RAF was transferred to Gamil airfield, which had been captured by the Parachute Brigade in their drop the previous day. There were also reconnaissance flights and liaison between HMS *Tyne*, the Command Ship, and other ships of the Task Group.

The expected losses of up to 10% of the helicopters did not occur, and because there were troops already on the ground when 45 Commando landed, they were able to deploy quickly and move westwards, fighting their way from block to block. The first assault landing of troops by helicopter from aircraft carriers had been successfully accomplished. At the end of the day, the helicopter force had landed 479 troops and 20 tons of equipment, embarked 96 casualties and made 194 deck landings. Casualties were usually located by the helicopter pilots, after visual sightings or by information gathered when landing and talking to the units on the ground. It was important that command and control allowed the casualties to be located quickly, even if last minute changes in the Landing Zone became necessary. The JHU evacuated 83 sitting and stretcher cases to the carriers on the day of the sea and helicopter landings, followed by a further 13 casualties the next day. Two officers and sixty men of the RAF Regiment, with their kit, were flown from *Ocean* to Gamil airfield. During the afternoon the unit's stores and vehicles were taken ashore in lighters, in preparation for the disembarkation of the whole unit on 8 November.[15]

At 1750 on the day of the landings, *Theseus* anchored at Port Said. The next morning the ship left harbour with the sad task of the burial at sea of Marine M J Fowler of A Troop, 45 Commando. He died of wounds inflicted the day before in a friendly fire incident involving Wyverns of the Fleet Air Arm, when their 20 mm canon shells ricocheted off the ground and the walls of nearby buildings, causing a number of casualties among the Royal Marines.[16] Later in the day, after a brief return to Port Said, *Theseus* left for Malta with 845 Squadron and 68 casualties on board. On arrival at Malta, *The Times of Malta* was able to report that 50 British and 18 French casualties were disembarked. Ambulances were waiting at the quayside to be hoisted by crane onto the carrier's deck. They were then driven to the lift and lowered to the after hangar, which was serving as a casualty ward. The ambulances when loaded were lifted back on shore, each man being given a ship's pennant as a souvenir. The wounded included Lt Col Tailyour, OC 45 Commando, who had been injured in the 'friendly fire' incident, together with Major HS Long and Lieut J C Weston. *Ocean* sailed for Cyprus on 8 November. She carried 30 casualties, including Egyptians, three of whom 'seemed to be between 12 and 15 years old.[17] Also on board were 574 officers and men of the 16th Independent Parachute Brigade.

845 Squadron soon reverted to its original anti-submarine role. Captain Shaw and Flight Lieutenant Stuart returned to the JHU in *Ocean* on 7 November. The Squadron disembarked at Ta'Qali on the island of Malta, where all aircraft were

refitted with their anti-submarine sonar and main checks carried out. The JHU Whirlwinds were dismantled at Akrotiri and flown home in Beverley transport aircraft of the RAF. They suffered from salt corrosion and were described as being 'full of Cyprus dust'.[18]

The objective of the airborne assault landing had been achieved despite considerable difficulties. The two helicopter units involved, 845 Squadron and the Joint Helicopter Unit, had not originally been formed with such an operation in mind. They had been called upon to adapt themselves and their machines at short notice from different roles. Training was intense with apparently good cooperation between the services. The variety of subsequent tasks performed by the helicopters and their crews showed their flexibility. British and French air forces provided complete air superiority over the assault area, and resistance from the ground was relatively light. Nevertheless, lessons could be learnt. It had been shown that a concentration of troops could be landed in a given area with 'speed and flexibility'. There would, however, be advantages in marking the LZ (Landing Zone) as soon as conditions on the ground allowed. Any helicopter reconnaissance before landing was time consuming, and could be hazardous as well as leading to a loss of surprise. There were communication problems, particularly when the JHU helicopters were dealing with casualties. Time did not always allow for control via the JOC; instead pilots often learned of the location of casualties by visual means or by direct contact with units in the battle area. Indeed, at times the casualties were evacuated from a place where there were no communications. The most effective communication had to be between pilots in the air. The VHF sets, fitted to their helicopters, provided voice communication within 'line of sight'. The limited frequencies available were difficult to change, when maintaining contact with *Theseus* and *Ocean*, other helicopters, and the ACT on shore.

The particular value of the carriers *Ocean* and *Theseus* was demonstrated, not only in their capacity to launch a helicopter assault from a mobile platform, but also by the variety of tasks the same helicopters were able to perform after the landings. An example was their ability to enable the airstrip at Gamil to be opened by landing key personnel speedily. However, this operational experience also showed that there should be limits to the demands placed upon the carriers. Launching an assault, troop carrying and acting as hospital ships were all within their capability, but satisfying one of these capabilities could seriously interfere with the effectiveness of another. For example, the thirty or so vehicles carried in each ship had to be stowed either on the flight deck or below in the one hangar available. But the helicopters needed to be stowed below to ensure full serviceability, and would need a clear flight deck when the operation began. It was fortunate in *Operation Musketeer* that such movements of equipment could be made in daylight and the weather remained fine.

The two carriers' responsibility for treating casualties brought its own problems. While the use of helicopters to lift casualties speedily from the battlefield for immediate treatment on board, including surgery, proved to be very successful, it was undesirable that troops waiting to be flown ashore and into action, should witness the sight of bloodstained comrades-in-arms being evacuated from the action. Whereas it might be generally claimed that morale is fortified by evidence of provision of care for casualties, the multiple role of *Ocean* and

Theseus in this case must have produced mixed feelings.[19] As the campaign was brief, the number of casualties fell within the capacity of the two ships to manage, and it was fortunate that *Theseus* had two army surgical teams on board and *Ocean* had three RAF medical officers. Space had to be provided for temporary wards, operating theatres and ablutions. The ships' companies, with typical concern for their comrades, scrubbed out the wards and gave blood. In future operations, the provision of a designated hospital ship would be essential. For Operation Musketeer, the Royal Yacht *Britannia* was requested but she was not made available. At the time of the operation in November, the designated hospital ship *Nevasa* was off the Cape of Good Hope, while two other designated Primary Casualty Receiving Ships, *Dunera* and *Dilwara*, were required as troopships.[20]

As a result of the Suez experience, in which the precise role of the helicopter assault was not determined until the last moment, lessons had to be learned. First of all, there must be time to perfect the briefing before the assault, and the duty of the first wave must be to secure or improve the landing zone. Planners should recognise that any future operation might be more seriously opposed, therefore fire support must be provided immediately before the landing. But of great significance was the speed at which the carriers could move to a given area of operations, in contrast to the slow progress of the landing craft assault convoys. Such ships, or future purpose built vessels, would be an essential component of any rapid deployment force.

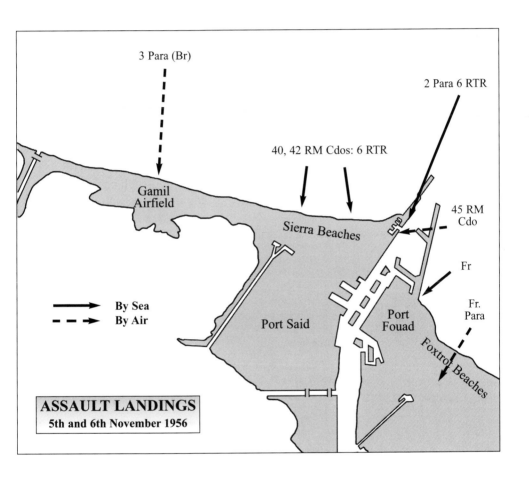

ASSAULT LANDINGS
5th and 6th November 1956

Chapter 5

Assault from the Sea

When General Sir Charles Keightley took up the appointment of Allied Commander in Chief of all British and French forces on 11 August 1956, he had already made plans for possible operations in the area while CinC British Middle East Land Forces. These plans were largely as a consequence of an Anglo-Jordanian alliance and could have involved action against Israel. Following Colonel Nasser's nationalisation of the Suez Canal the previous month, he then had to turn his attention to action against Egypt. Throughout August and September plans were made with flexibility the key word, since the precise circumstances of intervention could not be pre-determined.

In October, however, General Keightley was told to adjust his plans so that he could implement them at any time during the winter. In the meantime, he had identified factors that would limit such operations. He concluded that a seaborne assault could not be launched from Cyprus because of the lack of harbours, anchorages and 'hards' for landing craft. Therefore, his assault forces would have to sail from Malta, a distance of more than 900 miles. In the longer term, the limitations of Cyprus as a supply base meant that ships sailing with supplies for the assault forces would have to sail directly from the United Kingdom. These ships could not be held indefinitely under requisition in United Kingdom ports or in the eastern Mediterranean. Land based air support would also be limited: Nicosia airfield on Cyprus was already in operation but Akrotiri and Tymbou were still under rapid development. Air transport could only sustain two battalions and supplying them would present difficulties. The uncertain timing of any assault presented Keightley with further serious implications. His land forces contained a number of reservists who had already been serving for a lengthy period. They had been called up at short notice and it was unreasonable to keep them at short notice to move for a further possibly prolonged period without leave. Finally, the weather in the eastern Mediterranean could be expected to deteriorate during the winter months. General Keightley's conclusion was that ten days notice was required for the commencement of operations. He pointed out in his report on *Operation Musketeer* that in the event he was given 'little more than ten hours'.[1]

The forces available to the CinC were widely dispersed. Troops of the 3rd

Infantry Division were due to land in support of the assault force. They were in the United Kingdom and exercising on Salisbury Plain, while Commandos and the Centurion tanks of the 6th Royal Tank Regiment carried out landing exercises at Malta. The 10th Armoured Division, in fact a division in name only, was only up to the strength of an armoured brigade. It was based in Libya but, despite being held in extended readiness, it was withdrawn from General Keightley's command and took no part in *Operation Musketeer*. There was concern over the effectiveness of Command, Control and Communications and it was for this reason that *Exercise Boathook* was mounted, intended for November and to give the Headquarters ship in particular an opportunity for a Command Signal Exercise. In fact, when the ships sailed from Malta on *Exercise Boathook*, scheduled for 1-3 November, they were really on their way to carry out hostilities against Egypt.

On 30 October General Keightley was informed of the ultimatum issued to Egypt and Israel, requiring them to withdraw their troops away from the Canal and cease hostilities. In his report, he does not indicate any awareness of the collusion between Britain, France and Israel, but he would know that the ultimatum had been accepted by Israel but rejected by Egypt.[2]

For such an operation in 1956, an increasing mass of communications traffic had to be handled. For strategic messages, new technology was used via a high-speed machine using a separate code and transmitting to London by way of Cyprus. All tactical and day-to-day traffic was based on the Morse code, by which means messages were sent and received from the United Kingdom (Portishead), Gibraltar, Malta and Cyprus, and most of the large British and French warships engaged in *Operation Musketeer*.[3] For the Force Commanders, the focus of communications traffic was onboard HMS *Tyne*, the designated Combined Headquarters Ship. She sailed from Limassol on 4 November with the intention of being in position 30 miles off the Egyptian coast at the time of the airborne assault and so able to establish communication with the Parachute Brigade Commander.[4] As she steamed towards Egypt, the prospect of action thrilled the ship's company and 'made the atmosphere electric'. Following the successful parachute landings on 5 November, the ship secured off Port Said on 6 November, finally entering the harbour the following day and mooring close to the Western Breakwater. Throughout the last three days of the short campaign, Air Marshall Barnett conducted air operations from HMS *Tyne*, partly through the Air Operations centre at Episkopi, partly through daily directives to the Flag Officer Aircraft Carriers, and finally, when the airfield at Gamil was occupied, by direct orders to 215 Wing RAF. General Andre Beaufre, deputy to Lieutenant- General Sir Hugh Stockwell, the Land Force Commander, chose, with his staff, to remain aboard the ex-German depot ship *Gustave Zede* as his Headquarters Ship. Recognising that he was thus separated from the Force Headquarters in HMS *Tyne*, he nevertheless preferred to conduct French land operations from his own ship, especially as communications facilities aboard the British ships were already overloaded.

Captain Ronald de L Brooke DSO DSC* RN was appointed to Commodore in command of the Amphibious Warfare Squadron based at Malta. He flew his pennant in the LSH (Landing Ship Headquarters) HMS *Meon*. Brooke was not without experience in amphibious operations, During World War Two he took part in raids on enemy territory in 1941, the landings in North Africa in 1942 (*Operation Torch*), and later served on Admiral Lord Louis Moutbatten's staff at his headquarters in Kandy, Ceylon, as Forward Planning Officer for the projected landings on Japanese held territory in South East Asia in 1945. Brooke was also aide to Admiral Earl Mountbatten when he was CinC Mediterranean in the early 1950s. At Malta, a Joint Mounting Authority was belatedly set up just in time for the final loading exercise. During this exercise LCT(8) *Citadel* suffered considerable damage to her bow ramp while loading LVTs and had to be withdrawn from the operation. When all loading was completed the assembled Task Group 345.2 carried approximately 178 officers, 2,305 men, 51 tanks, 15 LVT, ten 17-pdr anti-tank guns, 19 scout cars and 479 other vehicles.

Midshipman Roger Weston, serving aboard the LCT *Bastion*, recorded in his journal an eyewitness account of the rising tension as ships at Malta prepared for sea.[5] On 27 October it had still been intended to carry out exercises the following week, then, on the following day, a Sunday, *Manxman* was seen to be hurriedly storing ship and preparing for sea. On that same morning the cruiser *Jamaica* raised steam and furled her awnings. Mail was collected. The international situation was described as 'a bit tense'. On 29 October the aircraft carriers, the cruiser *Jamaica*, two Daring class destroyers and frigates went to sea, while aboard *Bastion* the day was spent generally preparing for a lengthy period away from Malta. On Tuesday, *Bastion* and other ships of the Amphibious Warfare Squadron loaded, *Bastion's* load consisting of four 3-ton trucks containing reserve ammunition, four anti-tank guns with their towing vehicles, and a detachment from the 215th Field Ambulance. During the day the cruiser *Ceylon* entered harbour, having just completed an extended refit but not yet being fully worked up.

When loading was completed, the assault ships assembled outside Grand Harbour. At 2230 on 30 October the assault convoys sailed for Egypt, *Bastion* forming part of the convoy making up the British Assault Formation MES1. The eighteen ships steamed in three columns, 500 yards apart and were later joined on 5 November by the French contingent from Cyprus, made up of twelve ships in two columns.[6] The French escort included the battleship *Jean Bart* with her 15-inch guns. The weather was calm for the passage, never rising above Force 4. Changes of plan meant that Commodore Brooke had not been able to brief Commanding Officers before sailing, so this had to be done during the voyage east. Operational orders were opened and digested, while the fine weather allowed for transfer between ships of technical officers and ratings to repair breakdowns, usually in radar and electrical equipment. Intelligence and briefing instructions were also transferred while more routine signals traffic was conveyed visually. Valuable work was done by *ML 2583*, towed for much of the voyage by *Meon*, but used daily as a Duty Boat, carrying important correspondence. Some transfers were carried out by heaving line and by LST hauling ahead and lowering an LCA, activity that would not have been possible in bad weather.[7] The crews of the assault craft spent their time unpacking and reorganising stores in their vehicles. Guns were tested and the troops briefed on the coming operation about which, states Roger Weston, 'they knew nothing'.[8] Lt Commander John Pallot, a New Zealander, was sailing aboard his first command, *Salerno*. On his arrival at Malta, work up began with the rest of the

THE BRITISH ASSAULT CONVOY EN ROUTE TO PORT SAID
(Amphibious Warfare Squadron Operational Orders)

The French element formed two columns to port, joining at position 'UU'

11^	21^	31^	41^	51^
French Columns		*Striker*	*Meon*	*Suvla*
		Reggio	*Lofoten*	*Anzio*
		Puncher	*Bastion*	*Ravager*
		Salerno	*Buttress*	*Redoubt*
		Parapet	*Counterguard*	*Citadel*
		Rampart	*Sallyport*	*Portcullis*

Meon towed *ML 2583* in the above order, Formation 77, until Formation 77Y was ordered. Ships were in columns 600 yards apart, and the columns were 500 yards apart.

Meon

ML 2583

^	^
Striker	*Suvla*
Reggio	*Anzio*
Puncher	*Ravager*
Salerno	*Lofoten*
Parapet	*Redoubt*
Rampart	*Citadel*
Bastion	*Portcullis*
Buttress	*Counterguard*
Sallyport	

This formation (77Y) was to be assumed before arrival at position 'SS'. The two columns were four cables (about 800 yards) apart. The French assault convoy broke off to head for Port Foaud.

squadron, during which he had his only opportunity to practise a beaching. For *Operation Musketeer* his ship carried a mixed load including tanks, vehicles and 15th Field Ambulance, whose surgeons had hurriedly flown out from London.[9]

On joining Convoy MES1, the Flag Officer Flotillas and Support Group Commander, Rear Admiral D E Holland-Martin DSO DSC*, flew his flag in *Manxman* until he transferred to the cruiser *Jamaica* on the morning of 4 November. Although the convoy speed was planned for 6.5 knots, Rear Admiral Holland-Martin knew from recent exercises that landing craft of all types were susceptible to adverse weather conditions, and therefore it was sensible to make best speed eastwards while conditions were favourable.[10] He therefore called for 8 knots, but speed had to be adjusted during a period of 36 hours when the wind rose and the landing craft butted into a head sea. Aboard *Bastion* the changes of speed were assumed to be because of changes of plan, with the time of the assault being brought forward and then changed again. It was also noted on 3 November that the set of the tide was 1.25 knots westerly. Whatever the cause, the fact remained that the slow speed of the Amphibious Warfare Squadron prevented the troops from reaching their objective quickly. In this case, they could not have been seen to sail for an assault on Egypt before the expiry of the ultimatum delivered to Egypt and Israel. Nevertheless the lesson for any future campaign was that troops and equipment must be transported to the scene of operations at a much higher speed.[11] The passage of MES1 from Malta to Port Said was not entirely uneventful. There was a collision between *Salerno* and *Puncher*, the next ahead. Apparently, the landing ships were ordered to close to one cable distance instead of two, *Puncher*, in slowing down, struck *Salerno*, causing some damage to *Salerno's* bow doors. *Bastion*, too, had a moment of concern when cries were heard from astern and it was thought a man had been lost overboard. This was confirmed when *Sallyport* reported picking up a Royal Marine from *Bastion*. On 4 November the convoy met the US submarine *Hardhead* and signalled 'Good to meet you. Are you coming with us?' to which the reply was, 'No, am only holding your coat this time'.[12] That same evening, a patrolling Shackleton aircraft of the Royal Air Force sighted the US Sixth Fleet carrier force 30 miles east of the convoy.[13] The Shackletons provided distant anti-submarine support to the fleet carriers during the hours of darkness on 31 October, followed by similar support for the assault convoy MES 1 during daylight on 3 November. As the assault craft approached the beaches on 6 November, the Shackletons once more provided distant support, this time against the threat of Egyptian MTB attack mounted from Alexandria.

Holland-Martin had another problem. His other convoy, MES2, was made up of a motley collection of ships. The Commodore MES2's ship was the heavy repair vessel *Ranpura*, and his command included the RFAs *Wave Laird*, *Blue Ranger* and later *Eddybeach*, the tugs *Brigand*, *Careful*, *Energetic*, *Antic* and *Warden*, the salvage vessels *Sea Salvor* and *Kingarth*, the landing craft *Empire Gaelic* and *Empire Cedric*, and the armament carrier *Amherst*. *Wave Laird*, a diesel driven vessel, had difficulty steaming at less than 6 knots, whereas *Kingarth* would be lucky to achieve even 7 knots in a head sea. The consequence was that the two convoys, MES 1 and MES 2 drew further apart, eventually opening to some 60 miles.[14] To refuel the escort of convoy MES1, Holland Martin had to call *Wave Laird* forward early on 2 November to replenish *Manxman* and the destroyers *Chieftain* and *Chaplet*. He was saved from further difficulty when *Brown Ranger*, steaming to join MES2, missed the convoys, but found MES1 instead, enabling her to replenish the cruisers *Jamaica* and *Ceylon*, as well as *Manxman* and *Chieftain*. Having done her good work, *Brown Ranger* was sent back to MES2 at 1100 on 5 November, the day before the assault.

As the convoys steamed slowly towards their objective, a few members of some ships' companies were able to listen to the BBC and first became aware of the political divisions of opinion on British policy towards President Nasser's Egypt. This was becoming increasingly apparent in the House of Commons, where the opposition, led by Hugh Gaitskill, accused the Government of contravening the United Nations Charter. The division of opinion extended throughout the United Kingdom.

On the evening of 4 November, Holland-Martin learned that parachute troops would be dropped the next morning, the day before the planned sea landings. He realised that his speed of advance put him well ahead of the original timetable, and he could be in a position to launch the sea landing in swift support of the parachute landing if necessary. His proposal to this effect was not approved, so he reduced speed and returned to his original course.[15] It was on the evening of 4 November, when the British and French air strikes had been in action for more than three days, that suspicious contacts were made at 18 miles range. The convoy escorts turned onto a line of bearing between the convoy and the contacts. The Shackleton patrol could not identify the target, which eventually resolved itself into 5 ships. They were challenged at 5 miles to no avail, and although their movements did not seem like those of attacking Egyptian Motor Torpedo Boats, they continued to be challenged until a correct reply was received and the 'enemy' was revealed as five French auxiliary minesweepers. Rear Admiral Holland-Martin was not pleased at the failure in communication. In his report he stated: 'I destroyed the signal that I had drafted in case they proved to be British. It would have hurt more than a few rounds of 6-inch'.[16]

The Allied minesweepers now took up their positions to sweep ahead of their respective assault craft towards the shore. 6 November, the day of the sea landings was approaching. The minesweepers had to be prepared for mines off the entrances and approaches to Port Said and to Suez, with indiscriminate mining elsewhere. The threat of mines off Malta and Cyprus could not be ruled out.[17]

The Coastal Minesweeping Ships (CMS) in the Eastern Mediterranean comprised the 104th Minesweeping Squadron of 4 ships, the 105th, again of 4 ships, and the 108th with 12 vessels listed. The 108th M/S Squadron was based at Malta, and ship's companies had been contemplating a visit to Salerno when they became aware of staff officers hurrying from ship to ship, followed by the Captain of the Minesweeping Group (CTG 345.7), Captain J H Walwyn OBE RN, calling meetings of commanding officers. Something was afoot. During October, the ships carried out exercises before sailing for Port Said on the last day of the month. Nine ships of the squadron took up screening positions around their support ship, *Woodbridge Haven*, with Captain Walwyn on board. Progress was slow, normally at speeds between 5 and 8 knots, time being taken to practise firing with Bofors and Oerlikon guns as well as small arms. Replenishment at sea was carried out with RFA *Brown Ranger*. The ships eventually approached the Egyptian coast and became increasingly aware of intense air activity until, at dusk on 5 November, they observed the considerable fleet that had been assembled for the operation, a sight that one midshipman regarded as a fine target for an atom bomb. Overnight, the British minesweepers, having been joined by more 'Ton' class ships from Cyprus, rendezvoused with the French minesweeping force and took up their positions for the assault sweeps. Closed down and at Damage Control State One, they commenced their task of clearing a swept channel, some with wire sweeps, some laying dan buoys and some carrying out magnetic and acoustic sweeps. When they turned back off the beaches, no mines had been detected and the force could be almost certain that none had been laid. From their positions off shore, like the rest of the assault force they could see fires burning among the beach huts and the spectacular pall of smoke rising from burning oil storage tanks. In due course a channel would be swept into Port Said, with HM Ships *Sefton*, *Alceston* and *Leverton* leading the minesweeping force into the enclosed harbour.[18] With guns' crews closed up they moved through the harbour approaches, aware of the many aircraft zooming overhead, including helicopters from *Ocean* and *Theseus*. The fact that they were not attacked from the air confirmed that the aircraft must be friendly! Acting according to orders, *Woodbridge Haven* carried out the duties of Traffic Control Ship until she was relieved.[19]

While the minesweepers clearing the channel completed their work, *Darlaston* and *Letterston* of the 104th M/S Squadron embarked Clearance Diving Teams and a Joint Navy/Army Reconnaissance Team. Under orders from *Sallyport* they proceeded down the swept channel and entered the harbour. The two CMS were ordered to search the large ship berths for mines. The Clearance Diving Teams began their work at 0900Z and completed their searches by 1145Z. Again, no mines were found and further searches of ships' berths became unnecessary.[20]

By about 0900Z several of the minesweepers were secured to buoys, from which position they could observe destroyers giving close gunfire support to the troops ashore. Unfortunately *Sefton*, on entering the inner basin grounded on an obstacle. Although there appeared to be no damage or leaks to her hull, her propellers were damaged. The presence of the French LSD (Landing Ship Dock) *Foudre* enabled *Sefton* to be repaired after ammunition and fuel had been disembarked to lighten ship and enable her to enter the LSD. *Foudre* herself had to take on extra fuel to accommodate the minesweeper. On 11 November, several days after the cease-fire, new propellers were fitted in short time. It had been a difficult task as *Foudre* was designed to take flat-bottomed landing craft of under 400 tons and less than six feet draught. *Sefton* just about exceeded this, but she was also a round-keeled wooden vessel. Therefore a large number of keel blocks had to be secured to the bottom of the LSD and shores fixed into position. This entailed much hard work by the 'Chippies' from *Forth* led by the Senior Commissioned Shipwright Officer. Their hard work avoided *Sefton* having to make a long trip to Malta for repairs.[21]

The work of the minesweepers during the sea assault particularly impressed the Force Commander as they had the 'most intricate task to perform' under the SO Minesweeping Force.[22]

At 0230Z, having passed the 100 fathom line, the British assault ships assumed formation 77Y which involved a change from three columns to two. Ten minutes later the assault convoy split, the French turning away east towards Port Fouad, the British west towards Port Said. The British assault convoy was led by *Meon* with *ML 2583* steaming two cables ahead of the two columns of Landing Ships and Landing Craft. At 0400, on time, they reached the outer lowering position, whereupon, as ordered, *Striker* and *Reggio* carrying 40 Commando, and *Suvla* and *Anzio* with 42 Commando, proceeded on the same course to the inner lowering position. Here they launched out or lowered their LCA or LVT, before returning at their best speed to the outer lowering position. Royal Marines of 42 Commando headed for the right hand Green Beach, while men of 40 RM Commando took the left hand Red Beach.

It was originally intended that a naval bombardment should precede the landings with 15-inch gunfire from the French battleship *Jean Bart*, plus 6-inch shells from the cruisers adding to the salvos from the Darings and other British and French destroyers. Then, to avoid civilian casualties, orders were changed and Rear Admiral Holland-Martin now believed that his latest instructions required that there was to be no bombardment unless the Egyptians opened fire first. At the last moment he learned that the landing would be opposed and that land mines were to be expected on the beach. He expected further instructions, especially as it was well understood from World War Two experience that bombardment of the beaches was an essential prerequisite to an opposed landing. No instructions were received so Holland-Martin ordered drenching fire on the beaches by the four destroyers *Duchess*, *Diamond*, *Decoy* and *Chaplet* which preceded the landing craft. This action was described as giving 'supporting fire' to the landing and so distinguish it from a 'bombardment'. The four destroyers continued to steam ahead of the LST, engaging targets of opportunity and protecting the landing vessels. On arrival at the three-fathom line, they fanned out to port and starboard, two ships in each direction, and thus cleared their arcs to give full broadside support to the first and subsequent waves of landing craft.[23] *Decoy* set course and speed to lead the assault troops and then to give gunfire support. At 0403 she opened fire on Sierra Green beaches in support of 42 Commando. After the initial bombardment the ship anchored but was forced to move when fired upon by a gun located ashore. This target was engaged and possibly destroyed. Firing ceased at 0754 with *Decoy* having fired 457 rounds.[24] *Duchess* and *Diamond* fired 281 and 256 rounds of 4.5-inch respectively.[25] *Chaplet's* log recorded that the ship fired in support of No 40 Commando for 45 minutes from 0400 and thereafter fired as requested by the Headquarters Ship *Meon*, totalling 69 rounds from her main armament.[26] HMS *Chieftain* was ordered to silence any guns on the breakwater, but she did not open fire. At 0630 she was ordered to carry out the duties of Inward Traffic Control Ship. The cruisers *Jamaica* and *Ceylon*, circling further out to sea, were specifically told not to open fire with their 6-inch guns unless ordered to do so. *ML 2583*, appropriately manned by a Royal Marine Lieutenant and crew, laid a Dan buoy 1.5 miles from the beach and vectored the assault craft on their way to the beaches. The daylight assault prevented any opportunity for surprise, but it subsequently became clear that the assault forces were fortunate that guns on the breakwater close to the landing beaches, although well placed to enfilade the landing areas, had in fact been abandoned intact. The leading wave of each Commando heading for the beaches was carried in the Landing Vehicles Tracked (LVT) with the second wave going ashore from the LCA.

As the assault force approached Port Said, no lights could be seen from the shore but a cloud of smoke from blazing oil tanks hung over the city. Brigadier R W Madoc OBE ADC, commanding the 3rd Commando Brigade and standing on the bridge of the LCH *Meon* could see the British assault craft all around, with the French landing force visible further to the east. Just after dawn the first air strikes went in, targeting the beach defences and the western breakwater. Three squadrons of RAF Venoms from Akrotiri, despite heavy cloud, attacked emplacements on the western mole with rockets. Fleet Air Arm aircraft were soon on the scene and within ten minutes the strikes were over and the destroyers leading the landing ships had opened fire.

40 Commando (Lt Col D G Tweed MBE), in the LST (A) *Striker* and *Reggio*, headed for Red Beach, while 42 Commando (Lt Col P L Norcock OBE) made for green beach in LST (A) *Anzio* and LST (3) *Suvla*. The LVT were the first ashore, having 'lumbered out of the water and charged straight up and beyond the beach'.[27] They were followed by troops brought ashore in the assault landing craft. At H hour plus 20 minutes, the first waterproofed Centurion tanks were also ashore, six of them with each Commando. Brigadier Madoc landed just after the tanks and set up his headquarters.

The Commodore was able to report that the assault generally went according to plan:

> No craft broke down and communications organisations worked smoothly. All the LCA beached on time and in general with a lesser water gap than had been feared would be the case.[28]

The LVT, under the command of 3 Commando Brigade, were found to be particularly useful in bringing troops safely ashore from touch down to the back of the beach, even though the assault was not seriously opposed. These vehicles were used in conjunction with tanks, but the report states that 'they would have been more effective had their pin-on armour arrived in time'. The landing was carried out without casualties to men or craft. The timing of the landings was indeed fortunate, for by midday on 6 November the weather had deteriorated, and Commodore Brooke considered that for 'the next five days the weather was such that it would have been impossible to carry out the operation'. He also commented that the determination of the Commandos was 'an inspiration to all crews of landing craft'.[29]

The Centurion tanks of 6th Royal Tank Regiment were embarked in *Ravager* (A Sqdn), *Salerno* (B Sqdn), *Rampart*, *Redoubt*, *Parapet*, *Buttress* (C Sqdn) and the Regimental HQ and HQ Squadron in *Puncher*. After breakfast at first light, the troops went on deck to see 'an imposing array of shipping lying off Port Said and Port Fuad'.[30] They were then ordered to mount their vehicles thirty minutes before embarkation. At 0430 the LVTs assault craft, carrying the Commando assault waves, left their parent ships. The LCTs of C Squadron headed in line ahead towards the landing beaches, which were enveloped in a rising pall of smoke from burning beach huts and an oil storage tank. At 0508 the 14 tanks of 'C' Squadron, their crews having received the good news from 42 Commando

that the beach was clear of mines, clattered down the ramps into some 6 - 7 feet
of water 150 yards off shore. The Royal Marines had already taped their landing routes and the Centurions were soon in action repelling Egyptian counter
attacks. LST *Ravager* moved in towards the Casino Jetty followed by two other
LST and soon tanks were crossing the ramps to the shore. Tanks from 'A'
Squadron 6th Royal Tank Regiment landed at 0900 and reached the golf course
at 1015, being opposed only by sniper fire. They found the golf course boggy
in places, and three tanks were soon immobilised.[31] *Puncher*, having docked in
the Fishing Harbour, put No 2 Troop ashore. Even at this stage, a tank colonel
wished he could have got his tanks ashore earlier, so that they could have
advanced further down the bank of the Canal. B Squadron in *Salerno* was
brought into the Fishing Harbour, as was *Puncher*. Unfortunately *Salerno's* collision with *Puncher* while in convoy the previous night had damaged her bow
doors and there was a delay in berthing. The Officer Commanding B Squadron
reported that the doors of the LST had to be towed open by a beach armoured
recovery vehicle. Lt Commander Pallot's recollection was that his First
Lieutenant did not waste much time. He simply had a bolt welded on to the bow
door with a wire leading to a Centurion that quickly pulled it open. The first
vehicle disembarked at 1030. The Regimental HQ and the HQ Squadron, sailing in *Puncher*, were successfully put ashore as the ship docked in the Fishing
Harbour.[32]

The four Tank Landing Craft *Rampart*, *Redoubt*, *Parapet*, and *Buttress*, carrying the Centurion tanks of C Squadron, continued in line ahead until they
could lower their ramps and allow the tanks to wade ashore and give close support to the Marines. Unloading was completed in ten minutes.[33] When *Bastion*
and *Portcullis*, carrying first priority vehicles, reached the lowering position,
they detached from the main force and proceeded inshore, entering the main
fairway to the Canal. Midshipman Weston noted that the southerly wind was
blowing smoke out to sea from the burning oil tank farm behind Port Said. The
destroyers' gunfire had also set beach huts on fire. The two landing craft entered
the Fishing Harbour, berthing bow on. Both ships discharged their cargoes without difficulty, even though the front line was reckoned to be only about two hundred yards away. A single hand grenade from a Commando soon dealt with a
sniper in a pillbox on the southern side of the entrance to the Fishing Harbour.
The two ships then moved to the northern basin to await orders. Having landed
their assault cargoes, the landing craft assumed the role of ferries, transporting
troops and stores from ship to shore. *Portcullis*, for example, having discharged
her first load in some 27 minutes, slipped and lay off the harbour. At noon she
went alongside the troopship *Empire Parkeston* and loaded troops for the
Fishing Harbour. In the days that followed, the work of reinforcing and supplying the troops ashore went on.[34]

The LCT *Sallyport* had been converted into a headquarters ship 'with her tank
deck full of radio vans and her sides decorated with a plantation of swaying whip
aerials'.[35] With the protection of additional timber bulwarks and sandbags, she
had steamed at six knots as part of the assault convoy with the Amphibious
Warfare Squadron and the French Landing Vessels. On arrival off Port Said her
task was to lead the way into Port Said harbour itself once the minesweepers had
swept ahead. What would be awaiting them was uncertain, but intelligence had

suggested that there would be guns, mines and possibly Russian built tanks. The group was held up due to a delay in minesweeping. Sweeping ahead of the outer columns of landing craft was completed but it became clear that *Sallyport* would be late into the harbour and a request to go ahead was overruled. In the meantime *Bastion* and *Portcullis,* as already described, steamed gallantly and alone into the Fishing harbour. When the minesweepers at last appeared and swept ahead, *Sallyport*, one mile astern, led the way in at 8 knots, followed by the destroyer *Chevron* carrying the Naval Officer in Charge. In company were the two minesweepers *Darlaston* and *Letterston* with port clearance and diving parties on board, and the survey ship *Dalrymple*, destined to carry out an important role in clearing the wrecks from the canal entrance. There then followed the LCT and LST which, having launched their assault craft, now sought to unload men and machines inside the harbour. The difficulty was that the planned landing places were inaccessible because of the blockships sunk by the Egyptians. An alternative might be the Fishing Harbour, but it was thought to be too shallow to admit the LSTs. Fortunately, the diving team located a position close to the Casino Palace Hotel where the landing ships could discharge their tanks. Before dusk the deputy NOIC was able to report that five LSTs had berthed and lay ready to discharge their cargoes through the night. A complaint from the French that none of their ships had been called into the harbour to unload troops and equipment required a rapid response, as there were already rumours that a cease-fire might be ordered at midnight. By good ship handling, HMS *Reggio* completed unloading and cleared her berth quickly. Radio contact with the French ships proved difficult, but eventually they were located by an LCA butting its way through rough seas and one vessel was led into a berth near the Casino Palace Hotel. The British naval officer who had undertaken to pilot the French ship into harbour managed his self imposed task successfully despite being close to a wreck, the only damage being a glancing blow to one of two black-painted army LST nearby.[36]

Operational orders laid down the tasks for the landing craft after the initial assault. Twelve LCA were to report to the destroyer *Chevron*, the ship having secured stern on to the central mole. Volunteers from the ship's company manned requisitioned harbour launches for future use. Three small coasters had to be moved from the central mole by shore parties from *Chevron* and the tugs *Antic* and *Careful*. *Chevron* would still be flying a large blue flag. Their task would be to berth ships under the direction of the Naval Officer in Charge (NOIC), although crews might be required to form berthing parties ashore. The remaining LCA were to act as ferry runners. They were to report to *Sallyport*, with the Deputy NOIC on board, and receive their instructions from the Principle Beachmaster. *Sallyport* would, like *Chevron*, fly a large blue flag. Should any LCA be damaged, the Principle Beach master would decide what was to be done with the crews, though it was likely that they would support the berthing parties under the NOIC. Once the coastal minesweepers *Letterston* and *Darlaston* had searched the large ship berths for mines, and concluded that there were none, this allowed the troopships to be called to their berths at 1100. The troopship *Empire Parkeston*, carrying men of 16th Parachute Brigade, together with HMS *Theseus* were to be unloaded by LCA and LCT. Another troopship, *Empire Ken*, and HMS *Ocean* were also called in, but these ships were told to keep their troops on board until the army authorities were prepared to receive them.[37]

Once the troops were ashore, they became involved in street fighting and progress was slow, but by mid morning the situation was 'gradually being brought under control'.[38] It was then urgent to clear as much as possible of the Causeway running south from Port Said so that the port itself became available for men and equipment to be safely unloaded. By dusk, all organised resistance seemed to have ceased apart from the presence of some snipers.

At about 0900 a sequence of events began which could have had disastrous consequences for the whole operation. At that time Lieutenant General Stockwell reported to General Keightley that he was leaving *Tyne*, his head-quarters ship, to go ashore, where negotiations were apparently in progress that might lead to the surrender of Port Said. The French General Beaufre, who had just climbed aboard *Tyne* by way of the pilot's ladder in the absence of a gang-way, would accompany the other Task Force Commanders. In anticipation of surrender, therefore, this party of senior officers and members of their staffs, set sail from *Tyne* in a Motor Launch, heading for the offices of the Suez Canal Company. The Royal Navy party, including Vice-Admiral Durnford-Slater, was dressed in white uniforms and would have been particularly visible as the launch approached the harbour. As they approached the shore Vice-Admiral Durnford-Slater, determined that he should receive any surrender with his flag flying, had it duly hoisted above the launch. Lieutenant Fulford-Dobson, the Admiral's Flag Lieutenant, was standing with the others on the bridge of the launch, when he noticed a hole in the side of the bridge that he did not think was there a moment or two earlier. As he looked, a second hole appeared. The Allied Force Commanders were under sniper fire and a bullet ricocheted off the mast of the ML. While some of the senior officers flattened themselves on the deck, the Vice-Admiral, still standing, indicated to the young commander of the ML that their course ought to be reversed. It was only then that a message was received stating that the Canal Offices had not been taken. The ML then headed for the Casino Palace where the Commanders and their staff landed and headed for the Italian Consulate. There seemed to be a lot of noise and shooting going on. Vice-Admiral Durnford-Slater was then convinced that this was no place for an Admiral and returned to HMS *Tyne*. No surrender, however, was forthcoming.[39]

Having gone ashore, Generals Stockwell and Beaufre were not in effective communication with their headquarters, and remained so until after dark. General Beaufre has described how he eventually took leave of Stockwell and went to Port Fouad in a launch from *Gustave-Zede*. Having visited his troops and assessed the situation, he returned to Port Fouad. He might have remained there overnight, but since communications were faulty, he decided to return to *Gustave-Zede*, accompanied by his radio operator. Having ordered the ship to come inshore, he set off in a small boat, only to discover that the sea outside the harbour was rough and the night very dark. Only later did he discover that a false alarm of Egyptian or Soviet submarines being in the area had caused the dispersal of the Allied ships, with their lights extinguished and observing radio silence. He found his headquarters ship at last, after flashing signals, ending his venture with a steep climb up the pilot's ladder of *Gustave-Zede*.[40]

For General Stockwell, too, the day ended dramatically. Having decided to return to *Tyne*, he boarded a Royal Marine landing craft and ordered that he be taken to the flagship. Like Beaufre, he too found a heavy sea running and spray coming aboard. It was fortunate that Captain Bennett had decided to move his ship overnight so that she could enter harbour the next day. Having got under weigh, Captain Bennett said to the Admiral that he could see a winking light in the direction of the Gaza strip, and that he would head over and see what it was. As the 11000-ton flagship approached the position, the Royal Marine landing craft emerged from the darkness, having broken down. The coxswain of the boat thought that they could be swamped in twenty minutes. A jumping ladder was put out and a cold and sickly Stockwell and his ADC were brought aboard. They had in fact been adrift for about an hour and a half.[41] Lieutenant Fulford-Dobson recalled that the Admiral was not pleased, and expressed himself force-fully to the General, adding, 'My instructions to you are that you are never to leave my flagship unless I have personally supervised the arrangements for your return'.[42]

When the senior officers of the Task Force and their staffs were gathered on board *Tyne* in the early evening of 6 November, they heard via the BBC that a cease-fire had been agreed for 2359Z that night. This was followed at 1700Z, by orders from London, confirming the cease-fire and requiring the Allies to await the arrival of a United Nations Force. The message was received with sur-prise, and immediately General Stockwell ordered his troops to head off down the Canal as fast as they could to reach as far south as possible by the time of the cease-fire. General Keightly subsequently was able to report that his advanced forces had reached a position 23 miles south of Port Said, at El Cap. Given more warning of the government's intention, it seems certain that the Allied forces could have reached the southern end of the Canal. Their mission would then have been accomplished, but it would not have answered the question 'What then'?

The French Navy contributed to the naval forces supporting the amphibious operation. The 39,000-ton battleship *Jean Bart*, which had been the Gunnery Training Ship at Toulon, had a main armament of 15-inch guns and a secondary armament of nine 6-inch weapons. If required, she could bring considerable firepower to bear in support of the amphibious landings, and could also trans-port troops at high speed for rapid deployment. The 6-inch gun cruiser *Georges Leygues* had already been in action on 1 November in support of the Israeli army, by carrying out a bombardment of Egyptian fortifications near Rafah. On that occasion she attracted the attention of aircraft of the US Sixth Fleet. When the Allied landings took place neither *Jean Bart* or *Georges Leygues* opened fire in accordance with the decision to use only lower calibre guns. Egyptian casu-alties and damage to property had to be kept to a minimum. Other French ships supported their landings at Port Fouad, including the destroyers *Cassard* and *Bouvet*, and the destroyer escorts *Soudanais*, *Berbere* and *Touareg*.

The sea approaches to Port Said were soon crowded with ships. Apart from British and French warships that had taken part in the assault, there were vessels of both nations bringing support troops as well as motor transport, equipment, stores and victuals to sustain the forces ashore. Among them were the civilian manned LST *Empire Gaelic*, *Empire Cedric* and *Empire Doric*. The French hospital ship *La Marseillaise* entered harbour on 7 November followed in the next few days by the Fleet Supply Ship *Fort Dunvegan*, loaded with provisions, naval and salvage stores, the Heavy Repair Ship *Ranpura*, the Italian hospital ship *Ascania* intending to evacuate Italian civilians and, belatedly the Fleet Supply Ship *Fort Duquesne*, her lost propeller replaced. The RFA *Surf Pioneer* arrived with 10,000 tons of water. The troopships *Empire Fowey*, *New Australia* and *Asturias*, having sailed directly from the United Kingdom, arrived off the port on 10 November. They carried troops of the 3rd Infantry Division, commanded by General Churcher. Their arrival provided the opportunity for the relief of those units engaged in the landings and subsequent fighting. Men of the Royal West Kents, for example, disembarked from *New Australia* and relieved the 2nd Battalion, Parachute Regiment at El Cap, so enabling the Paras to embark for Cyprus on 12 November. Troops aboard *Empire Fowey*, however were not able to disembark for three days. Attempts to find a berth were unsuccessful and the ship had to enter and leave harbour on two occasions before eventually disembarking her troops on 14 November.[43]   On that same day, *Dilwara* arrived off Port Said and began disembarking troops into LST for transport to the shore.[44] In the week or so from the end of hostilities until the final withdrawal, the harbour was continuously under pressure to accommodate the waiting ships.

General Keightley now awaited either a renewal of hostilities by Egypt, in which case he intended to break out down the causeway to Ismailia, or alternatively, he must make preparations for the evacuation of the Allied forces following the arrival of the United Nations Emergency Force (UNEF).[45] The first UN observers soon arrived, followed after three days by the advance elements of the UNEF. *Operation Musketeer*, having led to the successful occupation of Port Said and the Suez Canal as far south as El Cap, was about to lead to *Operation Harridan*, the withdrawal of Allied Forces. By the time of the ceasefire, British casualties during the landings amounted to 16 killed and 96 wounded, while the French had lost 10 men killed and 33 wounded.

Chapter 6

Operation Toreador

In order to support operations in the Eastern Mediterranean, *Operation Toreador* was intended to protect British and neutral shipping approaching the Suez canal from the south, and destroy any Egyptian naval forces that might attempt to interfere with this traffic. The ships were to be prepared to bombard Egyptian shore batteries at the southern tip of the Sinai Peninsula, but this task was cancelled when it became clear that an Israeli armoured force was advancing down the coast of the Gulf of Aquaba. Task Force 324, activated to carry out *Operation Toreador* on 31 October 1956, was commanded by Captain J G Hamilton RN in the cruiser HMS *Newfoundland*, then only recently arrived at Aden from Singapore. His force was hastily assembled and initially widely dispersed. It would have to operate without air cover should Egyptian Air Force MiG fighters or Ilyushin bombers take action against it, and, in the course of operations, his ships could enter waters that had been mined. The frigates *Crane* (Captain B S Pemberton RN) and *Modeste* (Commander C E C Dickens RN) and the RFA *Wave Sovereign* (Captain W F Curlett RFA) were diverted from joint exercises off Trincomalee. The two frigates were originally built and commissioned as sloops of the World War Two 'Black Swan' class, being reclassified in 1947. They were well armed with six 4-inch guns as well as close range anti-aircraft weapons. *Modeste* had not been completed before the war ended, but *Crane* had a distinguished career, serving in the Mediterranean, in the English Channel during *Operation Overlord*, and in the British Pacific Fleet after the end of the war in Europe. In the long campaign of the Battle of the Atlantic she had helped in the sinking of two U boats, *U-538* in February 1943 and *U-962* in April 1944. Unfortunately, *Crane* had been in collision with *Modeste* during a night anti-submarine serial that had left the former with a damaged and crumpled bow. The ship continued in service after temporary repairs had been completed using steel plate and concrete. On 29 October, the two frigates, with *Newfoundland*, sailed from Aden towards the Gulf of Suez. Captain Hamilton also commanded the two French frigates *La Perouse* and *Gazelle*, and the coastal minesweeper *Jasmin*. *La Perouse* was ordered to remain at Djibouti, ready to embark troops if required, while *Jasmin* was asked to sail and rendezvous with the Royal Fleet Auxiliary oiler *Wave Sovereign*. The

British ships were warned to keep out of sight of land, especially as the coastal lighthouses might be in communication with Egyptian forces.[1]

HMS *Diana* (Captain J R Gower DSC RN) had left Singapore and was returning to the Mediterranean Fleet when she was ordered to join Task Force 324. *Diana* had been guard ship at the recent atom bomb tests in the Montebello Islands where she had been required to steam twice through the fallout from the two nuclear explosions. Now, having sailed from Aden, she joined the squadron on 30 October. It was the following day, when hostilities began, that orders to carry out *Operation Toreador* were issued. *Newfoundland* and *Diana* headed north at 20 knots with the remainder of the squadron following at their best speed but still far to the south. By evening the two ships were entering the Gulf of Suez. Darkness fell on a fine and cool moonless night, relieved by the lights of merchant ships which had to be identified. At 0103 on 1 November, when *Newfoundland* and *Diana* were in a position nine miles north of Ras Gharib, a ship was spotted astern of a group of merchant vessels. She was darkened apart from navigation lights, the position of which Captain Hamilton regarded as suspicious. The British ships were at action stations as *Newfoundland* altered course to pass under the stern of the darkened ship and brought up steaming parallel to the possible enemy on the starboard beam, 7 cables or about 1400 yards distant. *Diana* followed. *Newfoundland's* armament was trained on the target and ready to open fire. The ship's 20-inch signalling lamp illuminated the target, revealed as the Egyptian frigate *Domiat* (ex HMS *Nith*). Admiralty instructions required Captain Hamilton to aim for capture rather than a sinking, therefore he signalled 'Stop or I fire', which was acknowledged by *Domiat* as she appeared to slow down to 12 knots. *Newfoundland* then signalled 'Report when stopped', but at this point the frigate switched off her navigation lights, increased speed and trained her armament on *Newfoundland*. Believing his ship to be under threat, Captain Hamilton was forced to engage and at 0120 the cruiser opened fire with her main armament of 6-inch guns as well as her secondary 4-inch and Bofors. *Domiat* also opened fire with her 4-inch and close range weapons. The first British broadside struck *Domiat* on the waterline and the Egyptian ship was continuously hit as the range closed. At 0128 *Domiat* was seen to turn as if to ram, forcing *Newfoundland* to turn away and engage only with her after Y turret. At 0130 *Domiat* ceased fire and *Newfoundland* likewise checked, having fired nine broadsides. The cruiser had been hit by two 4-inch shells and close range fire, a Chinese steward being killed, and five of the ship's company wounded, none of them seriously. During the engagement *Diana* briefly engaged the target with her two forward turrets.

By now *Domiat* was on fire and sinking, capsizing at 0135 and remaining bottom up for about three minutes. *Newfoundland* lowered her whaler and picked up two men before getting under way in case a threat developed from Egyptian motor torpedo boats. *Diana* continued to search for survivors. Drifting down from windward and aided by the ship's whaler, six officers and sixty ratings were picked up, widely dispersed in what was described as a 'loppy sea'. After an hour and a half two unidentified ships were reported to the north west and Captain Hamilton ordered Captain Gower to hoist his whaler and join him 'with despatch'.[2] Regrettably this meant leaving a number of survivors in the water. Swimmers were still alongside the ship and there were at least two rafts in the vicinity. Captain Gower of *Diana* later described the scene as the action ended:

> The silence that followed the noise of the guns and the sight of the burning ship and the dazed men in the water all emphasised the destruction that can be wrought all too quickly by big, six inch guns. It was a sharp lesson to most of the ship's company........Any feelings of anger during the action were replaced by sympathy for the Egyptian sailors, many of whom had been trained in England.[3]

Many of the survivors picked up by *Diana* were wounded and gave the ship's doctor his first experience under battle conditions. The Surgeon Lieutenant from *Newfoundland* assisted him in giving treatment that included amputating the leg of one of the survivors. The wardroom was used as an operating theatre with other wounded being accommodated in the sick bay and the after galley. The prisoners seemed to be unaware that they were at war, and Captain Gower went so far as to observe that some of them wanted to join the Royal Navy as cooks and stewards, an offer which he had to decline. Some survivors from *Domiat* reported that their ship was heading south and carrying mines, 'thus indicating her intentions', when the British ships found her.

Diana's ship's company were sent to breakfast in four batches, and then during the afternoon, 55 survivors were transferred to *Newfoundland* by jackstay, leaving only the seriously wounded aboard the destroyer. On the afternoon of 2 November, *Diana* closed *Newfoundland* to take on fuel, a three hours exercise, during which the survivors were all transferred back again. It was necessary to land the prisoners as soon as possible as the ship was over laden and the heat intense. Conditions in the overcrowded destroyer cannot have been pleasant until the prisoners were finally landed at Djibouti on 6 November.[4]

Captain Gower's report stated clearly the conditions under which his ship fought. The ship's machinery worked well, the only failure being a repairable defect, but the condition of the hull, in its tenth month out of dock, limited the maximum speed that could be expected when ordered to sail 'with all despatch'. For the ship's company, inexperienced and with one hundred men under the age of twenty years, the event was 'stimulating', and their performance was a satisfactory outcome of three months training towards achieving fighting efficiency. The very few cases of neglect of duty were dealt with by suspended sentence, with but one exception. Everyone now understood the value of wearing protective clothing and lifebelts, and respected the necessity for damage control. Although the action had been very one sided, everyone gained in confidence in operating their machinery and equipment. *Diana* did not engage in further action with the enemy, but it was not until 24 November that the ship was ordered to return to Aden, having been at sea under war routine for four weeks. Their reward was to spend Christmas at Mombasa.[5]

Captain Hamilton signalled to CinC Mediterranean on 1 November that he intended searching for the Egyptian frigate *Rashid* (ex-HMS *Spey*). He also reported that the survivors of the sinking of *Domiat* had said that at first they believed *Newfoundland* was an Israeli warship.[6] The British ships remained alert, watching particularly for attacks by Egyptian motor torpedo boats. One such suspected attack developed after dark on 2 November, when *Newfoundland's* radar plotted a possible threat from three such boats. Over a period of two hours the 'attackers' were plotted and a chart drawn, but it proved a false alarm.[7]

The two frigates *Crane* and *Modeste* operated independently. *Crane*, with her crumpled stem, patrolled the approaches to the Gulf of Aquaba, while *Modeste* steamed off the southern end of the Gulf of Suez. Their responsibility was to continue to protect merchant shipping and search for any Egyptian naval vessels, in particular the frigate *Rashid*, thought to be in the Gulf of Aquaba. It was possible that this ship too was carrying mines. During this time, Israeli forces were moving south down the Sinai Peninsula. While at dusk action stations on 3 November, *Crane* was steaming into the Enterprise Channel, close to the mainland, and able to witness a battle raging ashore, with shellfire and movement amongst mechanised and armoured vehicles. Above the battle five aircraft were visible, flying low and dropping bombs. Suddenly they turned seawards and their attention focussed on *Crane*, despite the horizontal Union Jack painted on the fore bridge. The aircraft, initially identified as Egyptian MiG-15s, were then seen to be Israeli Mysteres. They headed for the British ship in line ahead at 45 degrees to the ship and launched rockets, possibly mistaking her for an Egyptian frigate. In response, *Crane* altered course, hoisted large battle ensigns and worked up to her full speed of 17 knots heading south east into the darkness of the approaching nightfall. Splinters from the rockets damaged both Bofors guns which had already opened fire, and injured three of the guns' crews. One rocket hit the ship amidships, puncturing an oil tank, one burst outside the depth charge magazine and one entered the wardroom from starboard and passed through the ship without exploding. The rockets were identified as anti-personnel weapons. Had they been armour piercing, the damage could have been much more threatening to the ship's safety. The Israeli aircraft continued to attack, first releasing small bombs that burst close astern, spraying splinters over the decks. In the second attack, one aircraft, under close range fire was seen to shed two pieces resembling cowlings, which fell near the ship. Then, on a third run, one of the Mysteres was seen to be hit and crash into the sea ahead of the ship, which then steamed past the smoke and flames rising from a patch of burning fuel. It is likely that a second Israeli machine crashed into the sea as a result of damage inflicted by *Crane's* gunfire.[8]

Despite *Crane's* damage, including severed power mains, the frigate carried out repairs during the night before steaming to join RFA *Wave Sovereign* and taking on fuel. This seemed to take an abnormally long time until oil was seen to be escaping from a ruptured fuel tank.

Subsequently, Leading Seaman Loader of HMS *Crane* was awarded the Distinguished Service Medal for his bravery in continuing to man his Bofors gun after he saw that he was the only member of the guns' crew still uninjured after the first attack. It must be assumed that the Israeli aircraft, like the ships of TF 324, were looking for the Egyptian frigate *Rashid* and thought they had found her. *Crane* continued to operate with the Task Force until departing for Singapore to pay off. As she steamed away, Captain Hamilton described her as:

> a fine sight, with her crumpled stem, her shot holes amidships and aft, her paying off pennant flying, and her ship's company in fine fettle.........I was sorry to lose her. She had carried out all her duties with zest and efficiency. [9]

The Commander of Task Force 324 signalled:

> Blunt in front,
> Holed behind,
> Pierced amidships,
> Never mind -
> You start your journey home today,
> And hell to Nasser anyway![10]

TF 324 had carried out *Operation Toreador* well. The large number of British and neutral ships heading south through the Gulf of Suez into the Red Sea had been picked up on the radar plot and identified. The one Egyptian warship had been rapidly engaged and sunk; threatened attacks by MTBs did not materialise, though there were some scares through misidentification by radar. The cruiser *Newfoundland* and the frigate *Crane* had suffered damage in action, but casualties had fortunately been light. There was no requirement to bombard Egyptian shore batteries before the cease-fire was called on 6 November.

Captain Hamilton and his ships of Task Force 324 had fulfilled their responsibility for the protection of merchant shipping in the Red Sea and the Gulf of Suez. Threats to his flagship had been met with decisive action, and the frigate *Crane* had responded vigorously when attacked, however mistakenly, by Israeli aircraft. No mines had been encountered, though intelligence was received that the Egyptians were laying mines at the Suez entrance to the Canal.[11]

Chapter 7

The United States Sixth Fleet

nder normal circumstances, the British and French naval forces might have expected support from the United States, not necessarily overt but at least through the absence of hindrance. The political situation that arose internationally and in the climate of an American Presidential election threw such support into doubt. There were differences of opinion within the Eisenhower administration, and in the Defence department. Admiral Arleigh Burke, United States Chief of Naval Operations, was of the opinion that the British and French actions against Egypt should be supported, and that what he called Colonel Nasser's 'international thieving' should not be condoned. Unfortunately for the Allied conduct of operations in the Eastern Mediterranean, the Secretary of State, John Foster Dulles, took an almost opposite view, suggesting that the crisis be met, if necessary, with the interception by the US Sixth Fleet of the British and French invasion forces. Therefore, when Burke signalled to the Commander Sixth Fleet Vice Admiral Charles R 'Cat' Brown on 31 October: 'Situation tense, prepare for imminent hostilities', it is not surprising that Brown should reply; 'Am prepared for imminent hostilities, but which side are we on?' Burke's forthright order to Brown followed; 'If US citizens are in danger, protect them: take no guff from anyone'.[1]

The Sixth Fleet was a powerful force. First established in the Mediterranean in 1950, it then consisted of two aircraft carriers, the 47,000 ton *Coral Sea*, capable of carrying up to 137 aircraft, and the 27,000 ton *Randolph* with some 91 planes, made up of Grumman Cougar F9F-8, MacDonnell Banshee F2H, and North American Fury FJ3 single seat fighters as well as Douglas Skyraider AD-2 carrier borne attack bombers. There were two cruisers, *Salem,* the Sixth Fleet flagship, a 17,000-ton ship with nine 8-inch guns and the 13,600-ton *Macon*, an older ship completed in 1945, but also carrying 8-inch guns. The big ships were supported by up to sixteen destroyers and two submarines, *Cutlass* and *Hardhead.*

The Admiralty was aware that an unfortunate and probably unintended incident could occur that might inflame relations between the United States and Britain and France. Admiral Earl Mountbatten, the First Sea Lord, had gone so far as to send a personal message via Admiral Grantham, CinC Mediterranean

Fleet. This message informed Admiral Brown, COMSIXTHFLEET, that British and French ships were operating between Cyprus and Egypt and of course wished to avoid any possibility of incidents between them and the US Sixth Fleet. He asked if it would be possible for Admiral Brown to discharge his duties by avoiding the area in which there were serious and imminent risks of an incident.[2] As early as 30 October, the French carrier force had reported meeting the US carrier group steaming at 20 knots. Admiral Grantham considered that danger was greater if US carriers were operating aircraft and US submarines were carrying out patrols. However, Admiral Power, Flag Officer Aircraft Carriers had already signalled on 31 October, that the Sixth Fleet, operating west of Cyprus, was an embarrassment in his neighbourhood. He had already twice intercepted US aircraft and there was constant danger of an incident. 'Can anything be done to keep them clear?'[3] His anxiety continued the following day, when, once again, he signalled that he was being 'bothered' by units of the Sixth Fleet. Occasional aircraft were encountered during the day, and, to make matters worse, the British carriers were badly hampered in the evening when recovering aircraft, by ships of the Sixth Fleet crossing their bows. These concerns were raised at the Chiefs of Staff meetings in London on 1st and again on 2nd November, when Earl Mountbatten reported that the Sixth Fleet was positioned between Cyprus and Egypt and 'aircraft were flying dangerously close to British warships'. He also announced that US submarines were operating in the area through which the assault convoys would be passing. They would therefore be able to report their movements and the date of the sea assault.[4] Vice Admiral Brown sent a personal message to Admiral Grantham wherein he hoped that precautions by all forces engaged in combat operations would avoid mistaken identity or other misunderstandings. He pointed out that his orders were to protect US nationals, including transport aircraft and surface transport for the evacuation and protection of their ships and aircraft from attack. He finally stated that US submarines were 'required to remain surfaced'. This last information seems not to have been fully appreciated, for, on 2 November the CinC Mediterranean was signalling that 'As US submarines may be dived after dawn on 2 November, submarines were not to be attacked unless showing hostile intent'. This introduced a dilemma on what, precisely could be interpreted as 'hostile intent'. Certainly a torpedo would, but what if a submarine was detected close to or within the screen? Such a situation arose on 3 November, when two periscopes were sighted and a sonar contact made near the helicopter carriers *Ocean* and *Theseus*. The ships were ordered to zigzag while on passage to the assault area off Port Said.

The presence of any submarines caused the Allied naval forces much concern, partly because identification would often be difficult, and any manoeuvre that was construed as a threat to Allied ships could well lead to an international incident. Rules of engagement were difficult to define when it was possible that submarines from Egypt, the Soviet Union or the United States of America might be involved. At first the Admiralty authorised attacks on 'unidentified submarines if operational requirements necessitates'.[5] While a threat from Egypt and the USSR was considered unlikely, at least two US submarines, *Cutlass* and *Hardhead*, were in the Eastern Mediterranean, and their orders were unknown. Efforts were made between the COMSIXTHFLEET and Admiral Grantham to prevent any unfortunate occurrence. The Task Group commander understood that the US submarines had established two patrol positions, thus enabling him to state that action would be taken against unidentified submarines located outside that zone after 2 November.[6] Some comfort was also drawn from a message on 1 November that all US naval surface forces would be fully illuminated at night.[7] In fact the submarine *Cutlass*, having armed its torpedoes, patrolled an area south of Cyprus, while *Hardhead*, also armed, patrolled a zone near Alexandria. Their orders were to observe events in their areas, to avoid other ships, to avoid action which could be misinterpreted as hostile, to maintain a speed of 10 knots and to identify themselves to other warships. Significantly, they were to remain on the surface at night with lights showing. Both submarines monitored air traffic in their areas.

Having received news of the British and French ultimatum, handed to Israel and Egypt on 30 October and due to expire the following day, three American ships, *Harlan R Dickson*, *Hugh A Purvis* and *Burdo*, designated TG 61.3, were ordered to Haifa to evacuate US citizens. The group arrived off Haifa at noon on 31 October. *Burdo*, a high-speed transport converted from a destroyer escort, entered the harbour and took on board 120 evacuees. She did not leave until after dark. Despite the blackout, *Dickson* embarked 46 US evacuees and some other civilians before the group sailed for Suda Bay Crete.

In the Egyptian port of Alexandria, the US Navy took control of the Export Line ship *Exochorda*. Some 300 evacuees were collected before the ship sailed for Naples the following day. Responses to the crisis by the US Navy extended further. The Sixth Fleet's amphibious forces were alerted and ordered to sail to Crete, where they embarked the Commanding General of the First Provisional Marine Force and his staff. The force consisted of five ships, USS *Pocono*, the Amphibious Force Flagship, the attack transports USS *Cambria* and USS *Chilton*, the LSD USS *Fort Snelling* and the attack cargo ship USS *Thuban*. *Pocono* and *Cambria* sailed to Turkey to pick up Admiral Walter F Boone, CinC US Naval Forces, Eastern Atlantic and Mediterranean who had arrived from his headquarters in London. The remaining ships headed south to Alexandria. At dawn on 1 November, when Allied air attacks began, three US Navy ships were anchored in Alexandria harbour. *Fort Snelling*, *Chilton* and *Thuban*, identified as TG 61.4, began taking evacuees on board. The Egyptians made their task more difficult by limiting the number of US Navy and Marine personnel allowed ashore to fifteen men. They were not allowed to carry arms and could not remain ashore after dark. Many of the evacuees came from Cairo, travelling along the Cairo to Alexandria highway in bus convoys while British and French fighter-bombers attacked nearby Egyptian airfields. Vice Admiral Brown had already informed Admiral Grantham on 31 October; 'US evacuees will be coming along the desert road from Cairo to Alexandria all afternoon 31 October and Possibly 1 and 2 November'.[8] Admiral Grantham replied on 1 November, 'Steps have been taken to ensure that evacuees are not endangered by attacks carried out by British and French forces. Request you inform us when evacuation of US nationals is completed and US ships are clear of Alexandria'.[9]

The evacuation covered two days and when the ships departed on 2 November they carried with them 1,056 adults and 480 children. Rumours that the harbour entrance had been mined proved false and Captain F W Laing, commanding the

Task Group, was able to signal the one word 'Outside'. Vice Admiral Brown, who had moved his aircraft carriers and cruisers closer to Alexandria to cover the evacuation, no doubt received this signal with relief. His ships remained out of sight of land, but their presence caused some hindrance to British and French warships, in particular the carrier groups, which had to manoeuvre in launching aircraft and landing them on. On 3 November a personal message to Admiral Grantham informed him that, on receiving word from the US Consul General at Port Said requesting the evacuation of the few United States nationals stranded there, he was sending the destroyers *Sumner* and *Sperry* of COMDESRON 16 to proceed there to evacuate them.[10] The message also stated that the evacuation phase seemed to be drawing to a close now that Alexandria and Cairo had been evacuated and the ships had cleared the ship channel. Vice Admiral Brown concluded that he would inform Admiral Grantham 'when transport aircraft and ships have cleared the area outlined by you'.[11]

Even as far away as Rotterdam, Rear Admiral Paul L Dudley, commander of Hunter Killer Group 2 aboard the anti-submarine aircraft carrier USS *Antietam* (30,000 tons), abandoned a planned reception on board for local dignitaries, and, on his own initiative, sailed for the Mediterranean on 30 October to join the Sixth Fleet. Leaving some of the slower ships to follow, the Group passed Gibraltar on 2 November.[12]

The French Navy was also subject to unwelcome attention from aircraft of the US Sixth Fleet. When the cruiser *Georges Leygues* headed close inshore to support Israeli troops on 1 November, she was the target of mock attacks by US Navy fighters.

Individual ships were forced to respond to perceived threats to their safety. The frigate HMS *Ulysses* reported on 2 November, that she had been 'continuously menaced in the past eight hours by US aircraft, flying low and as close as 400 yards. Two aircraft actually flew over the ship. The captain of *Ulysses*, Commander G H Peters, made a signal to the US cruiser *Macon*, 'Respectfully recommend your aircrew be briefed not to fly over or in the vicinity of British warships'.[13] Even as late as 4 November, the carrier *Bulwark* reported *Coral Sea* and two destroyers passing through Task Group 345.4 at 20 knots and exchanging signals.[14] Then on 6 November the submarine *Hardhead* was sighted by the Task Group and ships of the assault convoy MES 1. Once again, signals were exchanged. By this time, however, the main body of the Sixth Fleet had moved westwards for replenishment.[15]

Generally, Vice Admiral Brown had adopted a conciliatory tone. He had signalled to Admiral Grantham; 'Regret my mission required presence in this area at least temporarily. I have instructed aircraft carriers to minimum interference and submarines to remain surfaced. Have communicated your desires to my Government and earnestly hope circumstances will permit my withdrawal soon. I will advise.' Finally, on 5 November, Admiral Power was able to signal, 'Sixth Fleet drew steadily away yesterday and have ceased harassing me'.[16]

In his Summary of Operations During *Operation Musketeer*, Admiral Power described how, in the early stages of the operation, the US Sixth fleet operated very close to his carriers and that, on two occasions, *Coral Sea* and *Randolph* had penetrated his screen. While recognising that it was necessary for the American ships to cover the evacuation of American Nationals, he felt he would be placed in an impossible position if the US Government issued an ultimatum to the Allies to stop the operation. There was an ever-present danger of US aircraft being mistaken for Egyptian machines threatening the carriers, the consequences of which would exacerbate an already tense situation. Another consequence of US air activity was that it rendered the carrier group's air-warning radar 'virtually useless'.[17]

General Keightley, in his official despatch, published in the London Gazette of 10 September 1957, felt obliged to comment on the anxiety caused by the US Fleet operating close to the British and French carriers. He acknowledged that the US ships withdrew from the area during the night of 4/5 November, being clear of the parachute drop on 5 November and the sea assault a day later. He concluded that 'thanks to the good sense of the two naval commanders both were able to carry out their functions efficiently without incident'.[18]

Chapter 8

Operation Harridan and Opening the Canal

Hostilities officially ended at midnight on 6 November. Three days later General Keightley was instructed to retain the Allied hold on Port Said until a United Nations Force arrived. At the same time he must guard against any attempt by the Egyptians to breach the Cease Fire. In the changed circumstances, some redeployment of naval forces was necessary. Two British aircraft carriers and one French would remain in the Eastern Mediterranean, with other ships on picket duties off Cyprus. A force of minesweepers, with salvage and clearance vessels, would be employed in clearing the approaches to the Canal, with a small Red Sea force being based at Aden. The build up of land forces would continue, although the assault troops of 16 Parachute Brigade and 3 Commando Brigade would be withdrawn. Some support troops were still to be held in the United Kingdom, while their vehicles and equipment were waiting already loaded aboard ships at Malta. Shore based aircraft would remain at their present bases in Malta and Cyprus for the time being, although some Bomber Command aircraft would be held in readiness at their home airfields. The possibility of renewed hostilities with Egypt could not be ignored, in which case General Keightley intended to break out south down the causeway to Suez. He was concerned, however, that the Allies would be vulnerable to air attack if the Egyptian Air Force reappeared with aircraft supplied by the Soviet Union and its satellites. As in *Operation Musketeer* itself, high performance British and French fighters from Cyprus could still only spend about ten minutes over Port Said and even less further south. Air support, therefore, would continue to fall heavily on carrier-borne British and French aircraft. As in *Operation Musketeer*, the Fleet Air Arm fighters could again be at a disadvantage if confronted by MiG fighters, and once more the carriers themselves could become targets for any bomber force that might appear. Plans for the evacuation of allied forces must also be made, a contingency that became a reality when the British government agreed to the withdrawal of Allied units from Port Said as the United Nations Emergency Force assumed control. As General Keightley observed:

From then onwards our thoughts were entirely concentrated on evacuation which in itself raised many problems, the biggest being the fate of the Allied Salvage Fleet.[1]

The evacuation, codenamed *Operation Harridan*, required General Keightley to re-embark British and French forces from Port Said and Port Fouad in good order. Throughout the intervening period, he had to maintain security and keep a balanced force available to deal with any emergency. British and French plans had to be synchronised, especially in the management of shipping. The safety of the Allied troops were to be a priority, and had to continue until the last soldiers were safe aboard the ships. A period of 14 days was set as the minimum for the evacuation to be carried out, though it might be extended by as much as four days if necessary. No Egyptian forces were to be permitted to enter Port Said until the evacuation had been completed.[2] The scale of the task was evident from the presence of 13,500 British and 8,500 French troops ashore on 1 December, with a total of 4,400 vehicles and 10,000 tons of stores. They awaited the arrival of Norwegian, Danish, Indian, Yugoslav, Swedish and Colombian contingents of the United Nations Force. Throughout the whole period of the occupation, General Keightley had to contend with the fact that 'the Egyptians did their best to provoke incidents'. Local tradesmen were forced to keep their shops closed, yet bombs were thrown at military vehicles, and arms were smuggled into the area. Some casualties were suffered. As the withdrawal progressed, and the number of British troops fell to 7,000, all were concentrated within an inner perimeter, ready for the final stages. But it was not until 13 December that the day of the final embarkation was set for 22 December. On that day, the evacuation went smoothly and all the troops were aboard their ships by 1710. Some 20 minutes later the last ship cleared the harbour. Only a limited number of ships of the Allied Salvage Fleet remained, and they could only operate under the United Nations Flag.[3]

In the period between the cease-fire and the final evacuation, the two Royal Navy depot ships *Tyne* and *Forth* continued to perform important alternative roles. While the Allied forces handed over responsibility to United Nations troops, and efforts were made to remove obstacles and reopen the Suez Canal, these two ships remained at Port Said. On 8 November *Tyne* was still moored close to the Western breakwater, and continued her role as the Tactical Headquarters of the Joint Task Force, flying the flag of the Naval Task Force Commander, Vice Admiral L F Durnford-Slater CB RN.

HMS *Forth* was a submarine depot ship, and as such was normally commanded by Captain V J H Van der Byl DSC RN as commander of the First Submarine Squadron, but in fact she was commanded during the Suez operation by Commander the Hon T V Stopford RN. On arrival at Port Said on 7 November, she became headquarters ship of Captain E W Briggs DSC RN, the Naval Officer in Charge (NOIC) of the port. Commander L G Lyne DSC was the Queen's Harbour Master (QHM). During the afternoon of 7 November, the ship berthed near the Casino Hotel, and *Manxman*, flying the flag of the CinC Mediterranean, Admiral Sir Guy Grantham, went alongside her and remained overnight. The LST *Lofoten* berthed on *Forth's* port side and became responsible for the movement of the small assault landing craft (LCAs), which were used for clearing berths, berthing parties, taking pilots out to ships, evacuating casualties, and carrying personnel and stores. After dark, the LCA carried out anti-frogmen patrols and continued to do so night after night.[4] Apart from the ship's company, *Forth* housed a number of press and pilots of the Suez Canal

Company. She was able to assist in maintaining vessels in the harbour as they went about their wide-ranging duties. Water was provided for ships' evaporators, repair work was carried out on tugs, salvage vessels and merchant ships, assistance was given to the army ashore, canal light buoys were repaired and re-lit, bread was baked and distributed and the Fleet's mail was delivered. The ship's diving team was in constant demand.

Both *Tyne* and *Forth* had to adopt the condition 'Awkward State' to maintain vigilance against possible underwater attack. The ships' bottoms had to be inspected regularly and John Hard, then a 19 year-old National Service Able Seaman aboard *Forth* was one of those with responsibility as an upper deck sentry for dropping charges over the side to deter enemy swimmers. On one occasion his charge fell too close and, as Captain Fell described, 'a violent explosion shook the after end of the ship'.[5] The ships at Port Said remained alert against air attack, even though this did not materialise. Ships were ordered to assume 1st degree AA readiness at 1430 on 10 November and 'Air Raid Warning Red' was signalled at 1310 on 12 November, probably due to unidentified aircraft appearing on radar.[6]

HMS *Tyne* continued to carry out her command and communications responsibilities. Royal Corps of Signals personnel on board were reservists and therefore, understandably, out of practice in sending and receiving Morse; they were therefore employed on voice circuits. Telegraphists aboard *Tyne* continued as they had in *Operation Musketeer* itself. They had to handle signals originating from Vice-Admiral Durnford-Slater and his staff as well as those originating from Army and Air Force personnel aboard the ships. Traffic classified as Secret or Top Secret, including political material was routed via the Admiralty in London and prefixed with the word 'Terrapin'. Of course all secret and top-secret messages had to be encrypted, a necessity which caused delays.[7]

The commitment of other ships of the Royal Navy to operations in the Eastern Mediterranean did not cease with the end of hostilities late on 6 November. While some ships took on new duties, others continued as before. The fleet carriers *Eagle*, *Albion* and *Bulwark* still had work to do. Their role moved on to protect the shipping at Port Said and to be ready to launch strikes should the troops on the ground come under attack, either through the re-appearance of the Egyptian Air Force, or from Egyptian soldiers, whether in formations or disguised as civilians. When *Eagle*, with her catapults out of action, sailed for Malta on 7 November, Vice Admiral Power transferred his flag to *Bulwark*. But *Eagle* only remained at Malta for four days before leaving once more for the Eastern Mediterranean. In that time at Malta her catapults were repaired. Before her departure Admiral Grantham went on board to congratulate the ship's company on their performance during *Operation Musketeer*. Indeed, during November, a number of ships were visited by the First Lord of the Admiralty, Viscount Hailsham, and by the Force Commanders. The carrier squadrons settled into a routine. On reaching the waters off Port Said, *Eagle*'s 899 Squadron for example, put up two details of four Sea Hawks a day, while from 0530 to 1730 a division of four aircraft was kept at Condition Three, with crews briefed and available in the crew room for flying at 15 minutes notice. At this time *Albion* and *Bulwark* had been carrying out similar operations for ten days. The Combat Air Patrols (CAP) were airborne between the carriers and the Egyptian mainland, but did not cross the coast. The patrols sometimes took the opportunity to engage in formation aerobatics. With two carriers on station, this allowed one ship to be detached to return to Malta for replenishment of stores and recreation. The reduction in air cover was evident on 16 November when *Albion* entered Port Said 'for various reasons', *Bulwark* sailed for Malta and the two French carriers *Arromanches* and *La Fayette* left for Toulon and Cyprus.[8] When *Bulwark* lay briefly off Port Said, her squadron commanders met Admiral Grantham and were also able to go ashore. There they saw the damage inflicted by their air strikes, most notably by their rocket projectiles, and they were able to travel as far south as Kantara. On first returning to Malta, *Bulwark* had been at sea for three weeks. HMS *Albion* had a memorable visit from General Stockwell in mid-November. Members of the ship's company mounted a special Guard of Honour on the flight deck. They wore their uniforms and caps back to front and marched backwards to 'The Goons' chart success 'I'm Walking Backwards for Christmas'. On being invited to inspect the guard, General Stockwell obliged, entering into the spirit of the occasion by reversing his own cap. General Stockwell's visits were enjoyed, his visit to *Eagle* including a 'jovial and hearty speech, and thanks for the air support'.[9] On that occasion, the General and Air Marshall Barnett flew aboard by helicopter and, while Stockwell's forthright and uninhibited manner was appreciated it was noted that the Air Marshall did not commit himself on the relative value of RAF bombing and Fleet Air Arm close support.[10] The two commanders did, however, emphasise that despite all the parliamentary arguments over Suez, there had been no criticism of the armed forces.

The period between the end of hostilities and the withdrawal of British and French forces from Port Said was not without incident and tragedy struck twice for *Eagle*. On 19 November, the starboard outer gun of a Sea Venom in the ship's lower hangar was accidentally fired while the gun was being serviced, damaging other Sea Venom and Wyvern aircraft parked forward. One of the Wyverns caught fire and was a write-off, other damage being caused by fire, heat and salt water. Sadly, a naval airman was killed by the burst of fire from the gun. On 24 November a Skyraider of 849A Flight crashed into the sea, killing the crew of three. On a happier note, *Eagle* first embarked the six Whirlwinds of the Joint Helicopter Unit for Cyprus, their task successfully completed, and then on 28 November their six Sycamores were taken to Malta, having flown on from the airfield at El Gamil. The Sycamores eventually rejoined HMS *Ocean*, flying on just after the ship left Malta for the voyage home.

Unlike the fleet carriers, the helicopter carriers *Ocean* and *Theseus* did not remain at Port Said for long. On 7 November *Theseus* sailed for Malta with 50 British and 18 French casualties on board. Among the British wounded were men who had been the victims of the friendly fire attack on 6 November. The ship returned later and assisted in the evacuation of British troops. The next day *Ocean* sailed first for Famagusta, then on to Malta, having left Port Said with a battalion of the Parachute Regiment on board.

The LSTs *Suvla* and *Ravager* started a shuttle service between Port Said and Cyprus, while the fast minelayer *Manxman* continued ferrying passengers and fresh provisions over the same route. Three Army LCTs, *Arromanches* (L4086), LCTs *L403* and *L408*, manned by the Royal Army Service Corps (RASC) had sailed independently to Port Said. Having discharged their cargoes they, like Royal Navy landing craft, began ferrying men and vehicles ashore from ocean-going ships.[11] Other vessels used for the assault sailed away to Malta, *Salerno* leaving on 9 November and *Puncher* two days later. Lieut. Commander John Pallot, commanding *Salerno* recalls his encounter with the US Sixth Fleet on the voyage to Malta. To express his frustration with the activities of the US fleet during *Operation Musketeer*, he steamed ahead right through the carrier group 'without regard for their movements'.[12] Eight of the smaller Royal Navy LCT began ferrying men and supplies between ship and shore, until it was possible to negotiate the blockships and move into the inner harbour. The coastal minesweepers *Appleton* and *Edderton* sailed for Famagusta on 7 November to join three other 'Ton' class ships already there. The French minesweepers had already departed for Bizerta, North Africa, on 9 November, when four of them were ordered to return and so maintain a French presence. Finally, as the United Nations prepared to send observers, the LST *Striker* was sent to Haifa to collect them, returning on 13 November.[13]

For a time, the waters off Port Said and in the entrance to the harbour became extremely busy, crowded not only with merchant ships but also with vessels of the Royal Navy and the Royal Fleet Auxiliary. In the twelve hours extending from noon on 11 November to noon the following day, the Commander of Task Force 345 reported to the CinC Mediterranean that the following ships were at Port Said:

Tyne, Forth, Manxman, Meon, ML 2583, ML 1097; the cruisers *Jamaica* and *Ceylon* (about to rejoin the carrier group TG 345.4); the destroyers, *Daring, Chieftain, Chevron* (having completed her duties as headquarters ship of the NOIC Port Said), *Cavendish, Comet, St Kitts, Alamein*; the anti-submarine frigates *Undine* and *Whirlwind; Woodbridge Haven* and ten 'Ton' class coastal minesweepers of 108 Minesweeping Group; 13 LST and LCT, the heavy repair ship *Ranpura*, and the survey ship *Dalrymple* with salvage ships *Sea Salvor, Kingarth* and *Brigand*. The RFAs included *Eaglesdale, Tidereach, Wave Laird, Eddybeach, Brown Ranger, Blue Ranger, Surf Pioneer, Spapool, Spaburn, Amherst, Expert, Antic* and *Careful*. Out to sea on the same day, the carrier group TG 345.4 consisted of *Albion* and *Bulwark*, escorted by the destroyers *Armada, Barfleur, Defender* and the anti-submarine frigates *Ulysses, Ursa* and *Urania*. The RFA *Tiderace* and *Tidereach* supported the group. Further departures and arrivals were expected, including the LST *Puncher*, which sailed this day for Malta and then home with captured enemy equipment on board.[14]

Fort Dunvegan arrived at 0600 12 November with provisions, naval and salvage stores. With other ships at Cyprus and Malta, and at Aden, the weight of commitment in naval power was clear. Despite all the activity, on Remembrance Day, 11 November, the ships observed two minutes silence at 1100, the occasion being an opportunity, not only to remember those who had been killed in the two World Wars and Korea, but, more recently, to think of those who would not return from *Operation Musketeer*. One report stated that all ships at Port Said raised masthead flags at 0600 to celebrate France's National Remembrance Day.[15]

Although some British troops had arrived at Port Said after the cease-fire they held the positions reached by the Allies at the time until the UNEF took over and they were withdrawn as part of *Operation Harridan*. Destroyers and frigates provided defensive cover for the final withdrawal of British armed forces. Some destroyers would be present in the harbour, while LCA and Coastal Minesweepers would carry out harbour patrols. The French also covered their own forces' withdrawal, with destroyers remaining in the vicinity until loading was complete. On 14/15 December more than 11,000 British troops embarked aboard the troopships *Dilwara*, *Ascania* and the carrier *Theseus*, while others flew out by air. The troopships *New Australia*, *Asturias* and *Dunera* embarked further contingents. The Headquarters Ship *Tyne*, having fulfilled her extended duties transferred the staffs of Force Commanders to *Manxman* and *Dunera*, and took on board the British naval beach parties. French personnel were sent to *Claude Barnard*.[16] The last Allied troops prepared to leave Port Said on 22 December, the French leaving in daylight and the British overnight. Of the warships, HMS *Duchess* was the last to leave. Having been engaged on the Cyprus patrol, she had arrived at Port Said on 19 December, when Rear Admiral Holland-Martin went on board and inspected the ship. Having then gone alongside *Tyne* she later berthed in the harbour on 22 December. From there she observed the departure of the last British and French ships, including the French hospital ship *La Marseillaise* and landing craft, and the British *Reggio*, *Counterguard* and *Samsonia*. *Duchess* was in fact waiting in the hope that Lieutenant Moorhouse of the West Yorkshire Regiment might appear. He had been abducted and there was reason to hope that the Egyptians might have released him. He failed to appear and, at 2135, *Duchess* sailed, setting course and speed to enter the channel, then taking station three cables astern of the cruiser *Jamaica,* heading for Malta at 17 knots. Lieutenant Moorhouse had in fact died while being held prisoner.

As the last convoys steamed away, the fleet carriers *Eagle* and *Albion* were on hand to provide air cover. Skyraiders of 849 Squadron's 'A' Flight escorted the troopships away from Port Said and past the approaches to Alexandria, from which harbour Egyptian destroyers and MTBs might still constitute a threat. The patrols continued until the ships were clear of any possible hostile interference. Finally, as a boost to morale, *Eagle*, with her escorting destroyers *Cavendish* and *Barrosa* steamed through the nearest convoy.[17] It was Christmas Eve and only the ships of the Allied Salvage Fleet remained at Port Said. Over the Christmas period, ships of the Fleet were returning to Malta. On a rainy Christmas morning came *Duchess* followed by the carrier *Albion* and the cruiser *Jamaica* with a life size Farther Christmas tied to the bow jackstay. On her quarterdeck, the band played Christmas carols. Later in the day *Manxman* too returned to Malta. HM Ships *Tyne* and *Forth* entered the harbour on Boxing Day, *Tyne* still flying the flag of Vice-Admiral Durnford-Slater while *Forth* sported a large display of Father Christmas on a sledge hoisted between her funnels. Smaller ships, including a number of LCT, were still making their way slowly back to Malta, their job done.

Clearing the Wrecks.

While the maintenance of order and the restoration of the civil administration became the responsibility of the Allied commanders, high priority had to be given to salvage operations leading to the clearance of the wrecks sunk by the Egyptians.[18]   In the House of Commons on 6 November, the Prime Minister made the British position clear:

> Her Majesty's Government wish to point out, however, that the clearing of
> obstructions in the Suez Canal and its approaches, which is in no sense a military
> operation, is a matter of great urgency in the interests of world shipping and
> trade. The Franco-British force is equipped to tackle this task, and Her Majesty's
> Government therefore propose that technicians accompanying the Franco-British
> force shall begin this work at once.[19]

It had been foreseen before *Operation Musketeer* began that the harbour at Port Said and the entrance to the Suez Canal might be blocked and the survey ship HMS *Dalrymple*, the salvage vessel RFA *Sea Salvor* already part of the Mediterranean Fleet, the coastal salvage vessel HMS *Kingarth*, together with an ocean tug and four harbour tugs had accompanied the assault convoys. HMS *Dalrymple* (Lt Cdr J D Winstanley RN), a 1600-ton converted 'Bay' class frigate, had sailed from Tobruk to join the assault force in anticipation of survey work should the Egyptians succeed in blocking the Suez Canal. Having closed the heavy repair ship *Ranpura*, she was instructed on 5 November to join con-voy MES1. When the sea assault took place the next morning *Dalrymple* was ordered to set course and speed to follow the coastal minesweepers and the destroyer *Chevron*, entering the port at 0938. Later that morning a survey party left the ship, but it was not until 8 November that survey work really began.[20] By 9 November a channel had been marked through the blockships. More sal-vage vessels arrived during the next week and the first LST to pass through the blockships berthed in the inner harbour on 12 November.

A Suez Canal Operation Authority was set up on 17 November, responsible for clearance of the Canal. In charge was the French Contre-Amiral Champion with Captain Theodore Podger RN as his deputy. They were joined on 21 November by Captain W R Fell, a retired Royal Navy officer. He came in order to help lift the wrecks that blocked the passage through the Canal, eventually occupying what he himself described as a 'palatial cabin' aboard *Tyne*.[21] Commander John Moore had already undertaken the staff work for the task ahead. Contre-Amiral Champion, Captain Podger and Captain Fell met regu-larly to discuss progress. Captain Fell was a man of considerable experience. A submariner in 1939, he had later become involved in combined operations, the development of midget submarines and the Chariot (human torpedo) in Europe before heading for the Pacific.   On retirement, he was appointed by the Admiralty as a Grade I Salvage Officer, and successfully carried out a variety of tasks in this capacity before meeting his greatest challenge at Port Said.

The task facing the salvage teams was a daunting one. There were twenty list-ed wrecks between Port Said in the north of the canal and Suez in the south, including the ex-LST *Akka* that the Fleet Air Arm had attempted to prevent from

BLOCKSHIPS AT PORT SAID

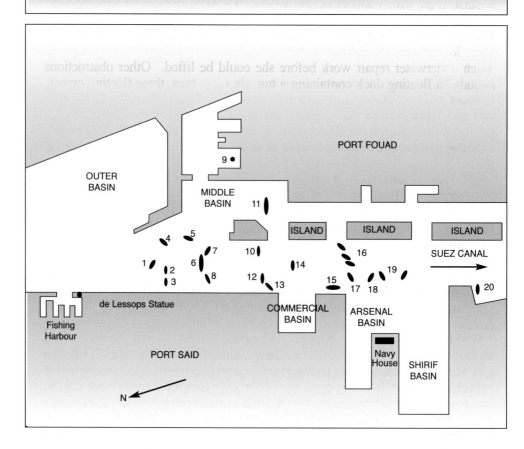

No		Type	No		Type
1.	*No 823*	150 ton crane	13.	*No 6*	dredger
2.	*No 827*	80 ton crane	14.	*No 19*	bucket dredger
3.	*No 839*	15 ton crane	15.	*Ardent*	tug
4.	*Pollux*	salvage craft			
5.	*Peleuse*	bucket dredger	16.	*Agile*	tug
6.	*Paul Solente*	suction dredger		*Cheddid*	tug
7.	*Neptune*	hopper		*Quircg*	tug
8.	*Triton*	hopper	17.	*Hercule*	tug
9.		floating dock	18.	*Le Hardi*	pilot boat
	Bassel	tug	19.	*Garii*	tug
10.	*No 37*	hopper 1		*Barq*	tug
11.	*Iacovos*	merchant ship	20.	*Actif*	tug
12.	*No 44*	hopper			

reaching a blocking position, and the frigate *Abikir* (ex-HMS *Esk*), ineffectively sunk in the main channel at Port Tewfik. Of more immediate concern were the numerous wrecks in Port Said harbour itself.[22] These harbour obstacles ranged from the 190-ton tug *Actif* to the 4,000-ton suction dredger *Paul Solente*. *Paul Solente* was the most seriously damaged by explosives and so required much underwater repair work before she could be lifted. Other obstructions included a floating dock containing a tug, six other tugs, three floating cranes, hoppers and bucket dredgers. Attempts to sink the vessels had been variously successful, but most of them constituted an obstacle to shipping. Four wrecks, salvage craft *Pollux*, a bucket dredger *Peleuse*, the merchant vessel *Iacovos* and a dredger, all lying clear of the channel, were ignored. No work was done on them.[23]

Lifting operations began at once. It was essential that a passage be cleared into the Commercial Basin, which provided the only suitable disembarkation facility for the army to land vehicles and stores. The boom defence ship *Barhill* worked at passing wires under the wreck of the 150-ton floating crane. She was later joined by two Lifting Craft, *LC10* and *LC11*, elderly vessels, properly equipped, but hastily manned for the operation and with crews lacking some of the skills and training needed for the arduous work ahead. The wreck of the 1,700-ton hopper *Triton* was also a hindrance to entering the Commercial Basin, but it was the first to be moved, once again due to the efforts of LCs *10* and *11* assisted by *Kingarth*.[24]

With the cease-fire having taken place, and the United Nations having become involved, there was a change in the management of the salvage operations. The UN Secretary General, Dag Hammarskjold, appointed Lt General Raymond A Wheeler, a retired US Army engineer to take charge of the clearance operations, and engaged two salvage firms, one Danish and the other Dutch. These companies formed the United Nations Salvage Organisation, known as Salvor. A considerable salvage force had already been assembled. By mid December fourteen British, three French, and two German Lifting Craft had arrived, with 11 more ships on their way through the Mediterranean. There were also eight ships at Aden and Djibouti. The coastal salvage ship *Dispenser*, civilian manned, arrived on 28 November with the floating crane *Retriever*. Naval personnel manned both ships. They first tackled the wreck of the 150-ton floating crane. Work progressed, hindered on occasion when the wind turned northerly, causing an uncomfortable swell to surge into the harbour area. When working inshore, houseflies invaded the salvage ships, causing a considerable nuisance to ship's companies until the offending insects were attacked with DDT. On 1 December *Kingarth* was joined by the newly arrived RFA *Succour* and began the task of removing the tug *Barq*. The boom defence vessels *Barhill* and *Barnstone* carried out various tasks from clearing moorings to sweeping lines under wrecks. They recovered fouled anchors, including that of the Cunard White Star liner *Ascania* that had come to Port Said to help with the withdrawal of British troops.

The practical work of clearing the Canal was regularly threatened by political wrangling between the United Nations, the Egyptians and the British and French. On more than one occasion this meant that resources were not used to the best effect. A case in point concerned the continuing uncertainty over the presence of mines. The minesweepers of 108 M/S Squadron were the most effective force capable of mine clearance, but once the United Nations had assumed responsibility for clearing the Canal, it seemed that they wished to use any force other than British. Certainly the Egyptians were very sensitive towards any British or French involvement, as they were seen as the belligerents. An example of this occurred on 17 November when three minesweepers, *Sefton*, *Dufton* and *Hickleton* attempted to sweep southwards down the Canal towards El Cap.[25] The ships were said to have been mistaken by the Egyptians for landing craft with the result that, following a request from the United Nations, they withdrew northwards. The Allies constantly argued that their salvage ships were vital for the efficient clearance of the wrecks. General Wheeler, however, asked simply for three Anglo-French ships to widen the channel through Port Said, with another six ships to work further south. These last six vessels were, however, to be manned by United Nations Salvage Organisation (SALVOR) crews. This was largely because the Egyptians would not allow Allied salvage ships beyond El Cap. The British Government was not prepared to hand over British ships without British crews, and furthermore, would not allow British ships to work in Port Said at all without British support being on hand. The Egyptians, on the other hand, would not allow British and French crews to continue their salvage work, as they 'would not be safe from the fury of the Egyptian people'.[26]

Matters came to a head when the salvage fleet, with many ships manned by civilians, decided to withdraw if they could not be sure of the protection of the White Ensign. The Admiralty was unhappy about this and told Admiral Durnford-Slater to try and persuade them to stay. Captain Podger and Captain Fell visited all the ships and the Admiral spoke to all the ships' captains. Admiral Grantham proposed that the ships should still be used but that they should fly the United Nations flag with their existing crews dressed in civilian clothes. Complicated negotiations followed. Civilian crews already manned some of the salvage ships, and some of them decided not to stay. Vice-Admiral Durnford-Slater successfully persuaded most of them to continue to serve. Those who still refused were replaced by naval officers and volunteer ratings who donned Merchant Navy uniforms. Officers had to provide their own clothes, while ratings were supplied from War Office 'demob suits' that had been sent to Malta or Aden.[27] Finally, it was decided that twelve salvage vessels would remain, with their support vessels. The salvage ships were the Royal Navy's *Dalrymple*, *Kingarth*, *Uplifter*, and *Barnstone*; the British RFA *Sea Salvor*, *Kinbrace*, *Succour*; the civilian owned *Salveda* and *Dispenser*; the French *LST 525* and two Lifting Craft, *LC10* and *LC11*. The support ships included the LST *Striker*, the RFA *Fort Duquesne*, *Blue Ranger* and *Spapool*, and the tug *Careful*.

The circumstances under which salvage operations were to be conducted changed on 22 December, when national flags were struck and United Nations flags were hoisted. It was a day not without incident. While the Anglo-French fleets were withdrawing, small arms fire with tracer bullets was aimed at Avant Port, where the salvage fleet was berthed. The firing continued throughout the night and into the next day. At first, only *Sea Salvor* and *Salveda* were allowed to resume work to raise *Paul Solente* and *LCT 525* was permitted to work again on the tug *Hercule* (Wreck 17). The Egyptians later stated that all the salvage vessels could work provided that *Dalrymple* and *Fort Duquesne* departed. This they did, *Dalrymple* leaving Port Said on 31 December, and *Fort Duquesne* on 3 January 1957.

Colonel Younis, Head of the Egyptian Canal Organisation, appeared as a constant thorn in the side of the British salvage crews. Having inspected the Fleet from a motor yacht on Christmas Day, he continued to hinder operations by complaining to General Wheeler that the salvage vessels were not flying the Egyptian flag according to international custom. Only the United Nations flag was flying. When music was heard coming from a British ship, it was implied that the men on board were slacking. It was still Christmas day! On another occasion a rating was given compassionate leave under the personal care of the UN General Wheeler. The man was then turned back by the Egyptian emigration authorities and only the General's personal intervention allowed him to fly home the next day. The pervasive atmosphere of suspicion caused CinC Mediterranean to make arrangements to support the British ships as necessary. On Boxing Day the new frigate *Torquay* and the anti-submarine frigate *Wizard*, recently converted from a destroyer, were stationed 25 miles north of Port Said in support of the UKSU (United Kingdom Salvage Unit); these ships were relieved by the destroyers *Cavendish* (D6), *Corunna* and *Barossa* on 29 December. The patrol was finally withdrawn on 4 January 1957. Although permission was given for six more salvage ships to resume work on 30 December, *Uplifter* and *Dispenser* were excluded and began a period of idleness until they sailed on 18 January. An attempt was made to put an Egyptian armed guard aboard the LST *Striker* at midnight on 30 December. This was the day when the Egyptians blew up the de Lesseps statue. The next day salvage ships were ordered to haul down the signal 'TE' (Go slow) as the signal flag 'T' 'looked French'. As *Barnstone, Kingarth, Kinbrace, Succour, LC10, LC11* resumed their wreck clearance, the survey ship *Dalrymple* sailed for Cyprus on New Years Eve, towing a lighter.[28]

It was not until 2 January 1957 that the tug RFA *Prosperous* brought the first mail to reach the salvage crews, but even then she was not allowed inside Egyptian territorial waters, the mail being collected by a small Dutch vessel arranged by General Wheeler. Similarly, mail arriving from Cyprus in HM Tug *Warden* was met outside territorial waters by United Nations officials in an Egyptian pilot launch. The run down of British vessels continued when RFA *Fort Duquesne* sailed for Malta, having transferred to *Striker* all the stores and provisions that could be of use. This was the day the destroyer patrol north of Port Said was withdrawn. At the end of the first week of the New Year some of the merchant ships trapped in the Canal began to move. The 1,200 ton tug *Hercule* was at last raised on 11 January and beached clear of the channel.

On this same day, the Canadian aircraft carrier HMCS *Magnificent*, Captain A B Fraser-Harris RCN, had 'entered the wreck cluttered harbour of Port Said and moored with two anchors forward and lines to two buoys aft'.[29] She carried 406 Canadian army personnel, 233 vehicles, four RCAF Otter aircraft and one hundred tons of supplies, all for the United Nations Force, and had orders to 'secure and supervise the cessation of hostilities'. The ship had been rapidly converted from her original role to provide accommodation for five hundred men, while

'B' hangar was filled with stores and equipment. Vehicles on the flight deck were the first to disembark the following day. Work below decks was carried out by the ship's company assisted by Finnish and Swedish troops, while other soldiers, including Indian troops, provided a security guard. Local labour was employed only on the flight deck and in lighters 'owing to their propensity for looting'.[30] The ship's Sikorsky helicopter carried out useful lifting tasks. Although twenty days had been allowed for unloading *Magnificent*, all United Nations stores were cleared in eight days, though the four Otter aircraft could not be flown off until 19 January, due to adverse winds. Limited leave was given and parties landed for trips to Cairo and the Pyramids, conducted as 'guests of the Egyptian Government'. This gesture shows the difference in the attitude of the Egyptian authorities to personnel operating under the flag of the United Nations compared with their firm objection to British and French involvement, in whatever capacity. One strange consequence of *Magnificent's* role under the UN flag rather than a warship of the British Commonwealth and NATO is shown by the experience of a British naval officer, Lt Commander Peter Wells-Cole, Staff Officer Administration to the Royal Navy portion of the United Nations Salvage Unit. His Senior Officer, Captain Podger, gave Wells-Cole a sealed letter to hand personally to the Commanding Officer of *Magnificent*. He went alongside the port accommodation ladder, but was stopped when he reached the top and was denied entry by the Officer of the Watch. Despite pointing out that he had a letter to deliver personally, that he was wearing a United Nations armband and that he was acting on behalf of the United Nations salvage unit, he was still refused permission to board the ship. The Officer of the Watch stated that he had been instructed not to allow any British Naval Officer aboard. It may have been that the Captain had been informed of Wells-Cole's presence, for he suddenly appeared, recognised Wells-Cole who had been two years his junior at Dartmouth, and took him down to his cabin. The letter was duly delivered and Captain Fraser-Harris apologised for the reception Wells-Cole had received, but he did not explain it. Not surprisingly, Wells-Cole felt humiliated by the experience, which seemed to him to reflect the opposition of the rest of the world to those who had engaged in *Operation Musketeer*.[31]

On 20 January, *Magnificent* finally sailed from Port Said for Naples, where the ship's company enjoyed a period of rest and recuperation. No longer representing the United Nations, the ship's next task was to proceed to the Clyde and take onboard 59 Sabre jet aircraft for transfer to Canada.

The wreck disposal work allocated to the British and French by the United Nations was completed on 21 January, including the heavily damaged *Paul Solente*, the largest blockship in the Canal. 13 wrecks, totalling 17,000 tons had been removed since clearance work first began on 7 November, the day after hostilities ceased. Almost immediately the salvage fleet began to disperse. After HMS *Dalrymple* and RFA *Fort Duquesne*, further departures followed;

12 January 1957	*Spapool* for Cyprus and Malta.
18 January	*Uplifter*, *Dispenser* having been idle for a month.
23 January	*Salveda* towing *LC10*, *Blue Ranger* towing two lighters, *Sea Salvor* towing a MFV, *Kinbrace*, *Kingarth*, and *Succour*, all sailed via Tobruk where they refuelled.

1. Royal Navy ships were a familiar sight at Port Said, either while on passage through the Suez Canal to the Far East, or as part of the Mediterranean Fleet. Here, in the 1920's the battleship *Iron Duke* lies at anchor, with a British India Steam Navigation Company liner astern. (*Author's Collection*)

2. Vice-Admiral R Durnford-Slater and staff in a photograph probably taken aboard HMS *Tyne*. To the Vice Admiral's right are Rear Admiral Lancelot, his deputy, and Captain J W M Bennett, Commanding officer of Tyne. To the left are Captain C P Mills, the Chief Staff Officer and his deputy, Captain Salmon. Captain Mills' opinion was that the French were co-operative and were 'extraordinarily good in recognising us as the senior partner'. (*Lt Cdr A Browne RN*)

3. General Sir Charles Keightley GCB GBE DSO, Commander in Chief of Allied Forces engaged in *Operation Musketeer*. On his right is Lieutenant General Sir Hugh Stockwell KCB KBE DSO, the Land Force Commander.   *(IWM MH 25376)*

4. HMS *Tyne* had a pivotal role in *Operation Musketeer*. Built as a destroyer depot ship, she was adapted to become the Force Headquarters Ship. She accommodated the three combined operations Force commanders. Arriving at Port Said on the day of the sea landings she remained, moored fore and aft, until 22 December, when British forces withdrew from Egypt.   *(Lt Cdr A Browne RN)*

5. HMS *Jamaica* was part of the covering force in the assault on Port Said, though she was not allowed to use her six-inch guns. Completed in 1942, she had a distinguished war record, most notably taking part in the sinking of the German battleship *Scharnhorst* in 1943. She served from the Arctic to the seas off North Africa and was also present as part of the British naval force in the Korean War.

(T. Ferrers Walker Collection)

6. HMNZS *Royalist*. This fine cruiser, regarded as the best-equipped ship in the Fleet to counter air attack, was forced for political reasons to leave the scene of action and head home to New Zealand. *(Maritime Photo Library)*

7. The cruiser *Ceylon* was completed in 1943. He battle honours included Sabang 1944, Burma 1945 and Korean 1951-52. Having just completed a refit, she sailed to the Eastern Mediterranean to replace the New Zealand cruiser *Royalist*.

(IWM FL 7813)

8. HMS *Theseus* at Malta in August 1956, en route to Cyprus with men and equipment of the 16th Independent Parachute Brigade. The ship sailed in company with *Ocean* and the cruiser *Cumberland*. *(T. Ferrers Walker Collection)*

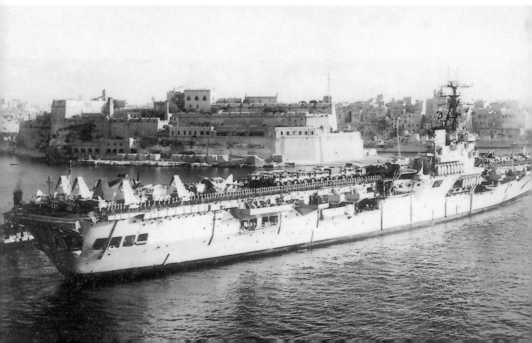

9. Grace and speed. The 'Battle' class destroyers *Armada*, *Barfleur* and *St Kitts* of the 3rd Destroyer Squadron, all played their part in '*Operation Musketeer*'.

(IWM FL 18467)

10. HMS *Woodbridge Haven* was completed as a Coastal Forces Depot Ship in 1945. From 1946 to 1954 she acted as a target for submarine attack, then in 1955 she became Coastal Minesweeper Headquarters Ship for the 108th Minesweeping Squadron. At Suez she fulfilled this role with Captain J H Walwyn OBE RN in command.

(Wickman Photographic Collection)

11. As a 'River' class frigate, H*MS Meon* served as an anti-submarine vessel in the Atlantic and English Channel in World War Two. She was part of the Royal Canadian Navy 9th Escort Group at Normandy in 1944. After the war she was converted into a Headquarters Ship for Combined Operations, and was already in the Mediterranean when the Suez crisis arose.   *(Wickman Photographic Collection)*

12. HM Submarine *Tudor* was completed in January 1944 and earned battle honours in Malayan waters in 1944/1945.   In 1956, the boat was part of the 1st Submarine Squadron in the Mediterranean, based at Malta, and seems to have been the only British submarine to take part in *Operation Musketeer*.
                                                    (Wickman Photographic Collection)

13. The troopship *Empire Parkeston* of 5,556 tons was built in 1930, serving during World War Two as an auxiliary cruiser and later as a landing ship under the name Prince Henry. As a troopship in 1956 she sailed for Port Said with *Empire Ken*. She later carried the 16th Parachute Brigade Group back to Cyprus, when they were withdrawn having completed their task. *(Wickman Photographic Collection)*

14. The British destroyer *Myngs*, renamed *El Qaher*, was one of two ships sold to Egypt in 1955, the other being *El Fateh* (ex HMS *Zenith*). The Admiralty succeeded in delaying their departure by refusing to allow their ammunition to be reloaded without permission. Captain Manley Power, Flag Officer Aircraft Carriers at Suez, had commanded HMS *Myngs* in 1944. *(Author's collection)*

15. Vice Admiral Manley Power CB CBE DSO* was Flag Officer Aircraft Carriers during *Operation Musketeer*. He flew his flag in the aircraft carrier HMS *Eagle*. Like many officers still serving in 1956, he had considerable war experience.

(MoD/Crown Copyright)

16. The aircraft carriers *Eagle* and *Bulwark* at Limassol in September 1956. The Suez crisis had already begun, but military engagement had yet to be ordered.

(IWM A 33605)

17. 'The Three Musketeers'. The Fleet carriers *Eagle*, *Bulwark* and *Albion* at sea in company. Their aircraft made a major contribution to air support in all phases of *Operation Musketeer*. *(MoD/Crown Copyright)*

18. Ready for action, HMS *Eagle*, flying the flag of Flag Officer Aircraft Carriers, steams at high speed towards Eastern Mediterranean waters. *(MoD/Crown Copyright)*

19. HMS *Albion* with her complement of Sea Hawks and Sea Venoms prepares for *Operation Musketeer.* *(MoD/Crown Copyright)*

20. Ground crew paint recognition stripes on the wings and fuselage of 800 Squadron Sea Hawks aboard HMS *Albion* before hostilities commence against Egypt.

(IWM A 33626)

21. 'Goofers' (spectators) on HMS *Eagle's* island look down on assembled strike aircraft already wearing the distinctive stripes to identify Allied aircraft throughout *Operation Musketeer*. In the foreground are Sea Venoms, then Sea Hawks and Wyverns with a single Douglas Skyraider at the after end of the flight deck. The same 'goofers' would have been ordered to disperse if the Wyverns had been about to land

(MoD/Crown Copyright)

22. Westland Wyverns of 830 Squadron, fully armed, prepare to take off from HMS *Eagle*. Two Skyraider airborne early warning aircraft are parked, wings folded on the flight deck, while a destroyer acts as plane guard close astern. *(MoD/Crown Copyright)*

23. Casualties arrive aboard a carrier for treatment on 5 November 1956. The Whirlwind helicopter is one of *Albion*'s ship's flight and the ship's log for that day records that a helicopter was flown off to fetch three wounded men. *(IWM G 5754)*

24. Sea Hawk WM 937 of 895 Squadron had a taxiing accident aboard HMS *Eagle* on 5 November when the port oleo brake failed. Other Sea Hawks are parked at the forward end of the flight deck. *(MoD/Crown Copyright)*

25. The Egyptian airfield at Dekheila under attack by Wyverns of 830 Squadron. It had been a Fleet Air Arm base, HMS *Grebe*, until March 1946. *(MoD/Crown Copyright)*

26. HMS *Bulwark* at Malta at the conclusion of *Operation Musketeer*. Her two Avengers are parked forward while her Sea Hawk Squadrons and members of the ship's company are assembled in immaculate order for inspection.

(MoD/Crown Copyright)

27. Lt Cdr Willcox brings his Sea Venom in to make a successful wheels-up landing aboard HMS *Eagle* on 2 November. His aircraft was damaged by flak in an attack on the Egyptian airfield at Almeza, severely wounding Flying Officer Olding, his RAF navigator.   *(MoD/Crown Copyright)*

28. Whirlwinds of 845 Squadron, Fleet Air Arm, lift troops of 45 Royal Marines Commando ashore from HMS *Theseus* on 6 November. Note the identification letters on the nose of each helicopter.   *(IWM A 33640)*

29. Royal Marines lifted by helicopter to reinforce the sea assault on 6 November, landed on an area close to the de Lesseps statue. A Whirlwind and a Sycamore of the Joint Helicopter Unit can be seen, as can army vehicles already ashore.

(MoD/Crown Copyright)

30. Sycamore and Whirlwind helicopters of the Joint Helicopter Unit aboard HMS *Ocean* at Port Said. The French hospital ship *La Marseillaise* is visible beyond *Ocean*'s 'island'.

(IWM A 33639)

31. The crowded anchorage at Port Said. The two helicopter carriers *Ocean* and *Theseus* together at Port Said with the troopship *Empire Ken* visible beyond them while the French LST *Cheliff* (L9006) steams towards the harbour entrance.

(MoD/Crown Copyright)

32. Five Sycamore helicopters of the Joint Helicopter Unit and a single Whirlwind fly over HMS *Ocean* at anchor at Port Said. The JHU transferred to Gamil Airfield after its capture by parachute troops.

(MoD/Crown Copyright)

33. HMS *Manxman* sailed from Malta on 30 October, flying the flag of the Flag Officer Support Forces, Rear Admiral D C Holland-Martin DSO DSC*. He later transferred to the cruiser *Jamaica*, while *Manxman* set course for Limassol. On 5 November *Manxman* took station ahead of convoy MES1 heading for Port Said.

(IWM FL 4456)

34. HMS *Decoy* at Malta. With the destroyers *Duchess*, *Diamond* and *Chaplet* she bombarded shore targets in support of the British landings on 6 November..

(Wickman Photographic Collection)

35. The French cruiser *Georges Leygues* was completed in 1937 and served with the Free French Navy in World War 2. Although she opened fire in support of Israeli troops on 1 November, she was not permitted to use her six-inch guns during the Allied landings at Port Said and Port Fouad. *(T. Ferrers Walker Collection)*

36. The French destroyer *Cassard* was one of a number of French warships acting in support of the French landings at Port Fouad. *(T. Ferrers Walker Collection)*

37. The Coastal Minesweeper HMS *Letterston* of the 104th Minesweeping Squadron passes the de Lesseps statue as she enters Port Said harbour. Helicopters can be seen bringing men of 45 Royal Marines Commando ashore to join the assault.

(IWM MH 23510)

38. Beneath a pall of smoke, landing craft manoeuvre close to the Fishing Harbour at Port Said, visible in the foreground. Coastal Minesweepers are also visible, having cleared a swept channel into the entrance of the Suez Canal. *(MoD/Crown Copyright)*

39. HMS *Bastion*, one of a number of LCT engaged in *Operation Musketeer*, formed part of the Amphibious Warfare Squadron. She successfully discharged her load at the Fishing Harbour, then was required to ferry troops and equipment between ships and shore.   *(Portsmouth Royal Naval Museum)*

40. The LST(3) *Salerno* entering Valetta harbour, Malta in September 1956. Brought forward from reserve, the ship carried tanks into the Fishing Harbour at Port Said on 6 November. Lt Commander J Pallot, a New Zealander, commanded her.
                                                                 (Portsmouth Royal Naval Museum)

41. The LCT(8) HMS *Redoubt* (L4001) carried tanks of 6 Royal Tank Regiment to Port Said. *(Portsmouth Royal Naval Museum)*

42. A Centurion tank of 6th Royal Tank Regiment disembarks from the LST(A) HMS *Puncher* on 6 November. *(IWM MH 23502)*

43. LST(8) *Buttress* disembarking. She first landed Centurion tanks on 6 November. The attitudes of personnel aboard ship and ashore suggest there is no immediate danger from enemy fire. She later lost her mast when it struck a sponson projecting from HMS *Theseus*. *(IWM MH 23500)*

44. Beyond HMS *Forth's* white ensign, the sea front at Port Said is busy. An assault landing craft is approaching the shore, while an LST, probably *Sallyport*, rests with her bow doors open. *(Courtesy John Hard)*

45. French coastal mine sweepers of the Acacia class gathered in the Fishing Harbour at Port Said. These wooden ships were transferred to France, from the US Navy, in 1953. *(Courtesy John Hard)*

46. HMS *Sefton*, having damaged her propellers on an obstacle in Port Said harbour enters the flooded dock of the French LSD *Foudre*. The presence of the French ship in Operation Musketeer enabled both propellers to be changed, thus avoiding *Sefton* having to return to Malta for repairs. *(IWM HN 94503)*

47. The cruiser HMS *Newfoundland* was completed in 1943. During World War Two she served in the Mediterranean, being torpedoed by the Italian Submarine *Ascianghi*. She joined the British Pacific Fleet in 1945. She underwent reconstruction in 1951/1952, emerging with distinctive lattice masts. During the Suez crisis she was the command of Captain J G Hamilton, Senior Officer of CTF 324 (Red Sea Force). In 1959 the ship was transferred to the Peruvian Navy as *Almirante Grau*.

(IWM FL 16761)

48. HMS *Dalrymple* was completed as a Survey Ship in 1949. On entering Port Said harbour on 6 November she was immediately required to locate wrecks sunk by the Egyptians, plan a navigable passage between the obstacles and initiate all necessary action. She was virtually forced to leave for political reasons on 31 December 1956, but her work under the command of Lt Commander J H Winstanley RN was much valued by those responsible for the disposal of wrecks.

(Wickman Photographic Collection)

49. HMS *Dufton* was part of the 108th Minesweeping Squadron, sailing from Malta on 31 October and responsible for sweeping, ahead of the assault forces, into the beaches and Port Said itself. The 'Ton' class ships became maids of all work, carrying mail and stores as well as transfers between ships. *Dufton* remained at Port Said until 22 November when she sailed for Famagusta. *(Author's Collection)*

50. HMS *Diana* was completed in 1954, the last of the 'Daring' class, built to traditional destroyer design. With HMS *Newfoundland* she engaged the Egyptian frigate DOMIAT. *(T. Ferrers Walker Collection)*

51. The 'Black Swan' class frigate HMS *Crane*, seen here at the Eastern Fleet Regatta in 1955. This little ship's determined reaction when attacked by Israeli aircraft earned the praise of Captain J G Hamilton, Senior Officer, Red Sea Force. *(IWM FL 25288)*

52. The French frigate *Gazelle*, 647 tons, was of a class described as 'robust, reliable and handy'. She served south of Suez under the overall command of Captain Hamilton in HMS *Newfoundland*. *(T. Ferrers Walker Collection)*

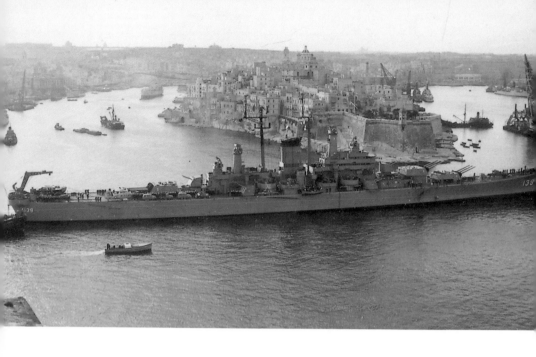

53. The heavy cruiser USS *Salem* was the flagship of the US Sixth Fleet in the Mediterranean. With her nine 8-inch guns, she was more heavily armed than any other ship in the Eastern Mediterranean apart from the French battleship *Jean Bart*.
(T. Ferrers Walker Collection)

54. *USS Allen M Sumner*, part of the US Sixth Fleet, was the class leader of an enlarged and modified design of the highly successful wartime 'Fletcher' class destroyer. These ships had a wide radius of action. *USS Charles S Sperry* was of the same class.
(T. Ferrers Walker Collection)

55. USS *Pocono* was an amphibious force flagship with facilities to act as a headquarters ship in combined operations. With *Cambria*, she was part of the Sixth Fleet's amphibious forces alerted at the time of the Suez crisis.

(T. Ferrers Walker Collection)

56. USS *Cambria*, 16,100 tons full load, was one of a fleet of Attack Transports commissioned into the US Navy. *(T. Ferrers Walker Collection)*

57/58. The depot ship HMS *Forth* is moored fore and aft with the LST *Lofoten* inboard. Beyond are LCT landing equipment and ships engaged in the removal of wrecks. *Forth* had a vital role as the headquarters ship of the Naval Officer in Charge (NOIC), Port Said. *(Courtesy John Hard)*

59. The Battle class destroyer *Barfleur*, with her battle ensign hoisted, closes HMS *Forth*. *(Courtesy John Hard)*

60. *Empire Ken*, the ex German *Ubena* (9253 tons) evacuated troops from Port Said to Malta and Cyprus as part of the British and French withdrawal. Her last trooping voyage was from Cyprus to Southampton. *(Author's collection)*

61. *Empire Gaelic* (ex LST 3507) was built in 1948. At the time of the Suez crisis she was one of a number of such ships chartered from the Atlantic Steam Navigation Co (known as 'Bustard boats) to transport equipment in support of the army ashore.
(Wickman Photographic Collection)

62. The Royal Fleet Auxiliary *Amherst*, seen here at Malta, was one of the ships that carried out a vital but unsung role in a maritime operation. Originally hired as the store carrier *Fort Amherst*, she was renamed in 1952. In the Suez operation she was a Naval Armament Carrier. *(Wickman Photographic Collection)*

63. The Joint Helicopter Unit transferred to El Gamil airfield, which had been captured by parachute troops in an airborne assault. Parachutes and equipment are still scattered on the ground. *(MoD/Crown Copyright)*

64. The frigate HMS *Wizard* refuelling at sea alongside an aircraft carrier. With the new frigate *Torquay* she patrolled off Port Said in support of the United Kingdom Salvage Unit after hostilities had officially ceased. *(Author's Collection)*

65. HMS *Striker* in Port Said harbour. This LST formed part of the assault convoy that landed troops on 6 November. After the cease-fire, she continued in support of the British land forces and then wreck clearance operations under the United Nations flag. She was among the last ships to leave Egypt, sailing for Malta on 24 January 1957. (*IWM FL 25883*)

66. Allied salvage vessels faced a complex task in clearing wrecks sunk in the Canal. It was a task frequently interrupted by Egyptian suspicions and negotiations with the United Nations Salvage Authority. (*T. Ferrers Walker Collection*)

67. The Mediterranean based Ocean Salvage Vessel *Sea Salvor* sailed in convoy with the assault vessels, and was present at Port Said from 6 November 1956 until 23 January 1957. She was heavily involved in the removal of the *Paul Solente*, the largest and most damaged of the wrecks in the entrance to the Canal.

(T. Ferrers Walker Collection)

68. The Coastal Salvage Vessel *Uplifter*, with two Lifting Craft, *LC10* and *LC11* and the Fleet Tug *Expert* at work removing the hopper *Neptune*. *Uplifter* was later prevented by the Egyptians from working and was eventually withdrawn on 18 December 1956, together with her sister ship *Dispenser*. The ships had been idle for a month. *(IWM MH 23561)*

69. The wreck of the Egyptian suction dredger *Paul Solente* was a major obstacle that had to be removed before passage into the Suez Canal could be opened.
(Courtesy John Hard)

70. The harbour and canal approaches at Port Said became busy with small craft commandeered by the Royal Navy. In the background HMS *Forth*, headquarters ship of the Naval Officer in Charge, fulfils her role as a 'mother ship'.
(Courtesy of John Hard)

71. An aerial view of the Ocean Salvage Vessels *Sea Salvor* and *Salveda* engaged in lifting the blockship *Paul Solente*.   *(Courtesy John Hard)*

72. *Operation Musketeer* is over but the task is not yet done. HMS *Albion*, RFA *Retainer* and a 'Battle' class destroyer in company in the Eastern Mediterranean on 11 November 1956.   *(IWM A 33618)*

73. Ships of the Royal Fleet Auxiliary carried out vital tasks to sustain the Fleet throughout *Operation Musketeer* and the following weeks when ships were continuously involved. RFA *Blue Ranger* was frequently at Port Said, refuelling vessels there. On 12 November there were more than twelve RFA vessels in the port. The captain of *Eddybeach*, Captain R T Mitchell, died, and was buried at sea on 12 December. *(T. Ferrers Walker Collection)*

74. The French *La Marseillaise* was the only designated hospital ship with the Allied forces at Suez. Beyond her, also at their moorings in Port Said, are merchant vessels requisitioned by the Admiralty. Two Ranger class oilers are also visible. *(Courtesy John Hard)*

75. The troopship *Empire Fowey* in Valetta Harbour, Malta. Astern of her, beyond the merchant vessels, lies HMS *Girdle Ness*. Built as a Landing Craft Maintenance Ship, she was converted for guided missile experimental trials, and commissioned as such in July 1956. Nearly a hundred firings of the British Sea Slug missile were fired between 1956 and 1958. Such weapons had a major impact on subsequent ship design and the conduct of naval warfare after Suez.

(Wickman Photographic Collection)

76. HMS *Fearless* was built in 1963 in recognition of the need for an amphibious capability in littoral warfare. Originally she was to be part of a balanced force East of Suez, but major changes in defence policy prevented this. *(Author's Collection)*

77. HMS *Albion*, after serving as a fleet carrier at Suez, was commissioned as a Commando carrier in 1962. In this capacity she operated off Brunei, Borneo and Aden. In 1971, when this picture was taken, she was engaged in the withdrawal from Singapore and the consequent disbandment of the Far East Fleet.

(Author's Collection)

24 January   *LCT 525* sailed for Famagusta, *Careful* towing *LC11*, and
                    HMS *Striker* left for Malta having first received mail from
                    HM Tug *Warden*. The tug then escorted *LCT 525* on her
                    voyage to Cyprus.

On the last day, General Wheeler, who had been given a most difficult task to perform, called on the remaining ships to give his personal thanks.

Throughout the whole operation to remove the wrecks from Port Said, the staff involved had to contend with changing political pressures, due in part to United Nations requirements, but mostly due to the sensitivity, indeed forthright objection, of the Egyptian authorities to any involvement by the British and French 'invaders'. The fact remained that the Royal Navy possessed considerable expertise in wreck disposal and without its contribution neither Egypt nor the United Nations could reopen the canal quickly. By foresight, salvage vessels had accompanied the sea assault convoys and so were on the scene when hostilities ended. The British team of Captain Fell and Captain Podger worked well, Fell being primarily concerned with the practicalities of wreck removal, while Podger took on what Fell described as 'the political and personal aspects'.[32]

The tense atmosphere created by the Suez operation was still evident, years later, when HMS *Ark Royal* approached the Canal at Christmas in 1963 at a time when President Nasser was due to give an anniversary speech on the Suez crisis at a nearby stadium. The ship's passage was delayed for a day and watch was maintained against underwater attack, including duty frogmen searching the ship's bottom for limpet mines. On entering the canal, wrecked ships were still to be found in the Lakes, some of them still resting on the bottom, having been there since 1956.[33]

Chapter 9

An Overview

In a democracy, the political decision to prepare for military action rests with the government of the day. Any United Kingdom government must make every effort to gain the support of other political parties in Parliament, and indeed the electorate as a whole, before embarking upon a military enterprise. It should also establish what support might be expected from potential allies. In the world of 1956 this required at the very least the acquiescence of one of the super powers, namely the United States of America or the USSR. Since the latter was seen by western democracies as the greatest threat to world peace through a possible nuclear war, it was the support of the USA that would be vital. For the United Kingdom it was also important to retain at least the sympathy of the members of the Commonwealth. Then, once a military option was a probability, the government's directive to the Chiefs of Staff should make clear the strategic objectives. The directive should not be subject to constant amendment, but should enable the appointed planning staff to proceed without ambiguity.

Unfortunately, the situation that existed in the Middle East was complex and volatile. There was a rise in Arab nationalism, matched by the aggressive determination of the state of Israel to assert its right to exist. Britain already had forces in Europe under NATO command, as well as garrisons in Cyprus, Hong Kong and Malaya. It also had treaty obligations in the Eastern Mediterranean, even though British troops had only recently withdrawn from Egypt. Then there was the concern over the safety of the nation's oil supply, not only in its production but also its freedom to pass through the Suez Canal. The days of the super-tanker, too big to use the Canal, had yet to come. So, when this freedom of passage for British ships was threatened, any British government would have to consider its response. When President Nasser of Egypt declared the nationalisation of the Canal in July 1956, the British Prime Minister, Anthony Eden, saw the action as that of the head of a dictatorial regime. Most of his political life as Foreign Secretary had been spent opposing such regimes, both politically and militarily. He was intimately aware of the consequences of appeasement towards Hitler and the failure to stand firm against Mussolini's aggression toward Abyssinia (Ethiopia). Now, as Prime Minister, his view was that Nasser must go, and if in the end this required military action, so be it. It was an emotional issue for him and he was not disposed to consider objections to it. What he failed to do was to gain and sustain the full support of his own countrymen, and convince his potential allies of the justice of his cause. In particular, he was unlikely to succeed without the support of the United States government, a condition that was not helped by the imminent United States presidential election due in November 1956. President Eisenhower, seeking re-election, was preoccupied with domestic issues and would not want to do anything that would appear to undermine the delicate peace that currently existed in an uncertain world. The Commonwealth, too, would have a say in any move by the British government towards hostilities of any form, as would the United Nations Security Council. This complexity meant that, while instructions may have gone to the Chiefs of staff to prepare for military action against Egypt, crucial political discussions must take place to give any such action a just *casus belli*. Finally, if British and possibly allied forces were to be sent against Egypt, the quicker the better. A *coup de main* might after all present the world with a *fait accompli* before any serious opposition could be mounted, both politically on the world scene and militarily in Egypt.

Once the Chiefs of Staff had received their directive to prepare *Operation Musketeer* against Egypt, they were immediately faced with the consequences of Britain having adopted a nuclear strategy. Although the British nuclear weapons system was small compared with the United States and the Soviet Union, it was expensive, and economic constraints on the defence budget did not allow Britain to maintain the necessary amphibious capability to mount a campaign quickly in the Mediterranean. Nevertheless the Chiefs' responsibility was to set up the command structure and organisation to carry out their instructions even though they were initially divided on the rectitude of the operation. Earl Mountbatten, in particular, was unhappy that they were being asked to plan a military operation against a small country, acting within its legal rights, and without the support of world opinion. The possibility of escalation could not be ruled out, with Russia having helped to rearm Egypt once the USA had refused to provide arms that could be used against Israel. But, in the end, the Service Chiefs were there to carry out the policy of the elected government. If only that policy had been consistent! Was the intention to depose President Nasser or was it simply to ensure safe passage through the Suez Canal by the ships of all nations? Whatever the objective, an amphibious operation of some kind would have to be launched, but where should it take place? Should it be Alexandria followed by an advance on to Cairo, or should it be directed initially at Port Said with the intention of advancing south along the banks of the Suez Canal? In either case, troops would at some point have to land in Egypt. Experience in World War Two had demonstrated the necessity for air and naval bombardment of beaches prior to any opposed landing. It was believed possible that Egyptian forces might be reinforced by 'volunteers' from Eastern bloc countries who would be familiar with Russian built weapons already supplied and so able to mount a stiff defence. For the planners, it soon became clear that any such attacks on Alexandria, including air and naval bombardment could lead to heavy civilian casualties. This was regarded as unacceptable. *Operation Musketeer* therefore was replaced by *Operation Musketeer Revise*, aimed directly at Port Said and the Suez Canal. It would begin with an air campaign to destroy the

Egyptian Air Force and, hopefully, overcome the will of the Egyptian population to resist. A landing was not therefore so urgent and might even be unnecessary. Such hopes flew in the face of experience, which showed that aerial bombardment alone tended to harden resistance rather than overcome it. An exception, of course, was the effect of the atomic bombs on Hiroshima and Nagasaki, but a nuclear attack on Egypt was not anticipated. Staff planning must still provide for putting troops ashore and taking control of the Suez Canal, even if this resulted in the Egyptians placing obstructions in the canal by sinking blockships.

In planning this operation against Egypt, a heavy burden fell upon the Royal Navy. Without strong naval forces it would be impossible to mount a campaign at all. The fact that the crisis had arisen in the Mediterranean was an advantage in the sense that the Mediterranean Fleet was still a major force, a command and control structure was already in place, and bases existed at Malta and Gibraltar. For the Navy, responsibility as Task Force Commander would fall upon the Flag Officer Second in Command of the Mediterranean Fleet (FO2). Vice Admiral Richmond held this post as the crisis developed, and was much involved in the planning. His time in the post was about to end, however, and it fell to Vice Admiral Durnford-Slater to take command only a few days before hostilities began. He must respond to late changes of plan and to see the operation through to a successful conclusion. At the end of the operation, he and his various Task Group Commanders would be in a position to present their reports, indicate lessons to be learned and give recommendations for future action.

Although *Operation Musketeer*, brief as it may have been, was conducted successfully, the importance of effective communications was constantly identified. Perhaps uniquely in military planning, the communications requirement is always immediate, starting from the moment an operation is projected. It has to be efficient at once with equipment and personnel at a high degree of readiness. To this end it is desirable that trained communications personnel should be provided from the active list, not from reservists who might need training. In 1956 much of the signals traffic was in Morse code, the efficient management of which demanded the highest level of skill. The full time Royal Navy telegraphists were best equipped to carry out this responsibility.

Both the Headquarters ships *Tyne* and *Meon* were regarded as inadequate.[1] Aboard *Tyne* the pressure on the recently fitted communications facilities was considerable, but this does not detract from the work of Lt Cdr R Durnford RN, the Fleet Communications Officer, who had compiled a Signals Communication Manual, a bulky document covering in every conceivable detail the various circuits and wireless frequencies believed necessary to control the Anglo-French naval, military and air forces. His Assistant Signals Officer was Lt Anthony Browne RN. Although much of the planning was carried out in Montague Annexe under the War Office in London, they later embarked in HMS *Tyne* before she sailed from Malta on *Operation Musketeer*.

HMS *Meon* in particular, showed serious shortcomings in an operation of the scale of *Operation Musketeer*. This was already understood, as it had been apparent during training.[2] The Commanding Officer of the Royal Marines was particularly critical of aspects of control in giving support to his men once ashore. The naval gunfire support team and the Air Control Team were satisfactory but there was no confidence in the 'centre' set up in *Meon*.[3] In particular, it was felt that fire support, controlled in *Operation Musketeer* by a Joint Fire Support Committee, should either be in the same Headquarters Ship as the command, or in a modern LSH(S) within VHF range of the Command Headquarters Ship. There was a feeling in 3 Brigade that, before *Operation Musketeer*, the JFSC spent a large part of its time in London, only moving to Malta for specific exercises, thus preventing thorough discussion with the units involved in the operation itself. *Meon* did not give adequate military briefing to the pilots of Cabrank aircraft available for close support. On the occasion of the 'friendly fire' incident on 6 November, the Wyvern aircraft strike leader believed that he was in contact with his ACT whereas he was in direct touch with the JSFC in *Meon*. It was because he thought he was receiving specific instructions from his ACT that he carried out the attack. It was noted that the call signs were similar.[4] It was this communications failure that caused 30% of the casualties suffered by the Royal Marines.[5] In any future operation on this scale a more modern and better laid out ship would be required.

For the first time in this kind of limited war, direct communications were established with a Rear Link in London. While valuable as a means of transmitting information to and fro, a consequence of this facility was that political interference with the conduct of the war became easier, thereby constraining the freedom of action of the commanders in the field.[6] There were certainly instances when General Keightley was asked to consider changes of plan at the last moment, interference that could have jeopardised a critical part of the operation.

Intelligence and communication are closely linked, since gathered intelligence, even if accurate, is of little use until it is communicated to those who need to know. This can best be achieved by ensuring that the Joint Intelligence staff passes information to the intelligence staffs in the theatre of operations, who must themselves work closely with the Force planners wherever they may be.[7] Of prime importance in planning an operation is an accurate assessment of the likely opposition. In 1956 it was known that the Russians had been rearming Egypt with aircraft, tanks and guns. It was thought likely that these weapons, notably the high performance Russian MiG and Ilyushin aircraft, would be manned by 'volunteers' from Eastern bloc countries. It was known that such 'volunteers' were involved in the Korean War. The presence of Russian built tanks, and self-propelled guns in concealed defensive positions could cause serious casualties to troops landing on the beaches. These threats did not materialise, but the assumption led the planners to prepare what has been called a 'mini-Normandy style invasion'.[8] Very surprisingly, and especially since the last British troops in Egypt had left only months earlier, information on the beaches chosen for the landings was 'meagre'.[9] Appropriate maps were apparently not available and the leading helicopters of the JHU, when required to land near the de Lesseps statue, did not know exactly where it was until someone recalled a postcard of the statue sent by a relative. An investigation into the existence of maps and charts that may have informed the Allied Forces would be a worthwhile study.

The presence of the three carriers *Eagle*, *Albion* and *Bulwark* was vital to the success of the operation. As floating airfields, they were able to use their mobil-

ity to sail close enough to the Egyptian coastal area for their aircraft to strike frequently and be less limited than the RAF aircraft from Cyprus, which could only
spend a short time over the target. *Eagle* as the single carrier in commission in
the Mediterranean before *Operation Musketeer* would not have been able to sustain the high level rate of sorties required to subdue the Egyptian Air Force on
the ground, support the landings when they took place, and provide air cover for
the fleet and convoys. Over the six days of action, it was possible for one carrier at a time to withdraw briefly for replenishment, the remaining two being
able to maintain the necessary pressure on the enemy. Two carriers would be
the minimum requirement for any future operation. It was a fortunate coincidence that the delay in the start of *Operation Musketeer* allowed the light fleet
carrier *Albion* to take part as the third such ship.[10]

The three British fleet aircraft carriers were handicapped by the unreliability
of the hydraulic catapults. Had the operation continued this weakness could
have seriously undermined the support given by Fleet Air Arm aircraft. As it
was, *Eagle* had to withdraw to Malta when her one remaining catapult failed,
while in both *Albion* and *Bulwark*, the performance of their catapults was
increasingly suspect. In his report, Vice Admiral Power referred to the unreliable catapults as an 'Achilles Heel' which caused him the utmost concern.[11]

Another weakness, which fortunately was not exposed by this operation, was
the aerial combat performance of the Fleet Air Arm fixed wing aircraft. They
were subsonic, and had they been seriously opposed in the air by MiG-15 and
MiG-17 high performance fighters flown by Russian pilots, they would have
been severely tested. All too frequently in the past, British naval aircrew had
been sent into action in low performance and often elderly aircraft, inadequate
to the task before them, only saved in the event by the morale, courage and professional skill of the crews themselves. An aeroplane may be delightful to fly
and even receive the affection of its crew, but in war it must be able to meet
opposition on at least equal terms and in adequate numbers. Stout resistance by
the Egyptian Air Force in 1956 could have prejudiced the whole operation,
reducing the effectiveness of the Fleet Air Arm Squadrons and even rendering
the carriers themselves vulnerable. In the ground attack role, the carrier borne
aircraft achieved considerable success, destroying much of the Egyptian Air
Force on the ground and attacking military targets. There were however, some
disappointments. Inadequate weaponry and combat inexperience were shown
by the difficulty experienced in destroying the Gamil Bridge, in destroying
coastal guns even though the gun crews had abandoned their posts, and in the
failure to prevent the ex LST *Akka* from being sunk in the channel and blocking
the Canal.[12] The pilots attacking the blockship and the bridge would have benefited from better intelligence. All that was known about the blockship *Akka*
was that it was about 3.5 cables south of the Canal company workshop in Lake
Timsah. Photographic evidence would have helped to determine the method
and direction of attack and even the number of aircraft to be deployed. A target
dossier on the radar site at Gamil showed the bridge, but there was no information on its construction. Such knowledge must have emerged after the parachute
drop, as the bridge was the objective of the Royal Engineers element. The eventual destruction of the bridge was due largely to the evidence brought back by
the one or two Fleet Air Arm aircraft on each sortie briefed to obtain photo-

graphic cover. It seems that, although the RAF carried out photographic reconnaissance sorties, very few images of value reached the Carrier Task Group.[13]

In welcoming *Eagle* home after Christmas, Earl Mountbatten wrote personally to Captain Maclean congratulating him and his ship's company on the part
they played in *Operation Musketeer*, adding that *Eagle* was the linchpin on
which the whole operation depended and it was hard to see how it could have
taken place without her.[14]

The aircrew of the piston engined Corsairs and Avengers operating from the
two French carriers had to be content with aircraft more obsolete than their
British allies. Nevertheless, Vice Admiral Power considered that they did
remarkably well once air superiority was certain. The Corsairs were particularly effective in strikes against shipping and ground targets.

In any operation of this kind, the effective management of the Underway
Replenishment Group assumed critical importance. In *Operation Musketeer* the
carriers' replenishment group operated some 30 miles north of the carriers themselves, and Vice Admiral Power described how ships were detached to refuel or
replenish every night and sometimes during the day. This required knowledge
of the state of ships in the Task Group and of the fuel, ammunition and other supplies in the replenishment ships. The coordinating role of the frigate placed in
charge of the Replenishment Group therefore became particularly important. A
shortage of Fast Replenishment ships was, however, exposed. Two such ships,
RFA *Retainer* and *Resurgent* had been purchased in 1952 and prepared for a
replenishment role. They were due for further conversion in the autumn of
1956, but events delayed this until the summer of 1957. *Retainer* was nevertheless of value during *Operation Musketeer* in carrying out RAS with ammunition and air stores. Ships of the Fort class, though classed as Fleet Supply
Ships, only had limited RAS capability.[15] Fortunately the Admiralty already
owned a fleet of tankers. These vessels, although available for charter when not
required for naval purposes, could soon be brought into service. Nevertheless,
despite all the difficulties, the immediate demands on logistic support were met.
The fact remains that hostilities only lasted a few days and therefore there must
remain doubt over the preparation and shortcomings that might have emerged
had fighting continued and had losses been incurred among the ships involved.
The distance from shore bases might have made afloat support more difficult.
The carriers, for example, had to return singly to Malta for repairs and replenishment. A prolonged campaign would have required more supply ships. Other
commitments, notably the atomic tests in the Pacific (*Operation Grapple*) would
have necessitated the requisition and conversion of ships, a lengthy procedure.

The use of *Ocean* and *Theseus* to fly off troop carrying helicopters was perhaps the most innovative part of *Operation Musketeer*. As with the fleet carrier
Albion, it was fortunate that these two ships were able to take part. Fully
equipped Royal Marine Commandos were successfully landed in a key position
within a few minutes of take off from ships that were capable of bringing them
to the scene of operations at high speed. The two ex-light fleet carriers were
mobile and independent of shore bases, but they were required to carry out other
duties in addition to operating assault helicopters. This was unsatisfactory, and
in any case these two ships were unlikely to be available in the future.

Before *Operation Musketeer*, the low priority given to the use of helicopters in an assault role meant that there had been no adequate training sufficient to establish a technique.[16] They were eventually called upon at relatively short notice as a reserve to those troops who had already landed by sea. The ground was therefore already held by British forces, though the first attempt at landing was met by enemy fire. No helicopter was lost in the assault and casualties were far fewer than anticipated. Vice Admiral Sayer, in his report, recommended that in an unopposed landing, the Landing Zone (LZ) should be marked out to avoid waste of time in reconnaissance and possible loss of surprise. If an opposed assault was expected, then fire support should immediately precede the landing, and the first wave of troops should secure the LZ. Most importantly, to avoid a repetition of the constant changes initiated from London, such an operation must either have been studied beforehand, or at least time must be given to perfect the necessary briefing.[17] The helicopters used in *Operation Musketeer* were not ideal for the task. Both 845 Squadron Whirlwinds and the JHU aircraft, partic- ularly the Sycamore, could only carry a small number of men in uncomfortable and exposed positions. A more robust helicopter with greater lifting capacity would be needed if a rapid deployment force were to be created. The 22 heli- copters used in *Operation Musketeer* were of different types and the provision of spare parts was inadequate.

In addition to their assault role, helicopters also showed their value in the rapid evacuation of casualties from the battlefield to hospital facilities aboard the car- riers. It was not, however, recommended that the helicopter carriers should try to combine the role of troop carrier and hospital ship. Troops following up an assault and waiting to be lifted into action might well be disconcerted to witness the arrival on deck of seriously wounded comrades. Fortunately, in this brief campaign, casualties were lighter than might have been expected. When, short- ly before noon on 6 November, following the sea landings, *Manxman* approached the helicopter carrier *Theseus* to take on casualties for transfer to Cyprus, she was informed that there were not enough. *Manxman* therefore went on to Limassol.[18] Vice-Admiral Sayer also commented that better liaison might have enabled French wounded to be taken straight to the French hospital ship *La Marseillaise*, lying at Port Said only a short distance from the British ships.

After an evaluation of the helicopter borne assault, the role of the helicopter in the Royal Navy extended beyond an anti-submarine role to include squadrons tasked with lifting assault troops in amphibious operations. This new role was secured soon after *Operation Musketeer* by the decision to convert two aircraft carriers into commando carriers. The two ships chosen had already played their part in 1956 in a fixed wing role. *Bulwark* was commissioned as a Commando Carrier in 1960, followed by *Albion* in 1962.

Preparing for and carrying out the sea borne assault most exercised the inge- nuity of the planners, for the ships to carry it out were not available. Response to the crisis was therefore much too slow. As the report on the conduct of oper- ations stated:

> The main conclusion that can be drawn from the assault side of this successful operation is that if we require to have , a 'fire brigade' ready to deal with the con- flagrations that are liable to break out suddenly, it is no good waiting for the fire to start before pulling the fire engine out from the back of the barn. Like its coun-

terpart ashore the fire engine must be polished and ready and the crew handy.[19]

Mobilisation plans and the Order of Battle that existed for a Global War were not intended for an operation such as that required at Suez. Although the Mediterranean Fleet included a small Amphibious Warfare Squadron, the run down in amphibious forces meant that it was inadequate to carry out anything larger than a raid. Only one Commando Brigade could be lifted, and certainly the necessary follow up required to reinforce an initial landing could not be sustained. No adequate Headquarters Ship was available. For the amphibious assault, ships had to be brought forward from reserve. Although they were 'prepared and steamed to their dockyard ports with commendable speed'[20] they still had many defects, repairs to which must be balanced against the time required to bring them and their crews to a satisfactory level of efficiency.[21] In the end the number of LST was 'just sufficient', but none of the troopships carrying personnel could carry LCA. Instead LST(A) had to carry men and so limit the lift of vehicles. It was argued that the operation would not have been possible had it not been for the seven LST chartered from the Atlantic Steam Navigation Co, and not all of these ships had been stiffened to carry Centurion tanks.[22] In future, if a force the equivalent of two Commandos were to be landed, then sufficient landing craft must be available at short notice, even though some could be in operational reserve. Modern LVT (Landing Vehicles Tracked) would still be needed. In mounting and sustaining an amphibious operation, the correct loading of ships was particularly important. Equipment should be loaded in the same ship as the personnel intended to use it. It was unacceptable that medical units and some engineers should become separated from equipment immediately necessary to their operational needs.[23] It was noted that the presence of the French LSD (Landing Ship Dock) *Foudre* showed that such a vessel would form a useful part of a future Amphibious Warfare Squadron. *Foudre's* ability to dock the coastal minesweeper *Sefton* and repair her propellers showed her value in the forward maintenance of small naval ships and Landing Craft.[24]

The commandos of 40 and 42 Royal Marines Commando carried out their amphibious landings successfully and with few casualties. The beachhead was secured and tank support forthcoming. In support, 45 Commando landed from helicopters in the first operation of its kind. But important deficiencies were revealed. Before the operation, no Royal Marines Commando was immediately ready and trained for an amphibious operation. The specialist shipping required for a rapid response, and many of the vessels eventually made available, were elderly and generally too slow. In the future, it was recognised that there should always be one Commando available with recent amphibious experience, with a more balanced and modern squadron of suitable ships to transport them rapidly to the scene of operations. In any amphibious operation, effective communications was essential, with all three services working to co-ordinate and disseminate intelligence, as well as carrying out combined exercises. In 1956 information all too often failed to reach those with a need to know, or was misleading and misunderstood.

While it may be unwise to allow a particular campaign to become a template for future planning, these are lessons that should have been learned from the

Suez campaign of 1956. Since then, the advance in the speed of communication world wide, where the media, particularly television, expose every move to public scrutiny, has determined that there must be a strong moral case for military intervention. Political and military objectives must be clear, and political will to initiate action and see it through to the end increasingly demands public support. Allies remain essential and wider international understanding still strongly desirable. The delay in mounting *Operation Musketeer* undermined all these necessities, allowing British public opinion to weaken in its support, and, even more critically, world opposition to grow until it became intolerable. Then the threat of Soviet intervention through 'volunteers', or even the outbreak of an atomic war, combined with the threat to the pound sterling forced the British Prime Minister to agree to an immediate cease-fire. It is easier to start hostilities than it is to end them, so it is wise to have an 'exit strategy' and be clear on the means by which hostilities might be terminated.

Once the political decision has been made to take military action, the deployment of the necessary forces must be carried out quickly to prevent the crisis from developing. To this end the opening phase of a campaign should be, if possible, decisive. This in turn requires that the forces exist for rapid deployment. For the British, it was always likely that any deployment would be a considerable distance from the United Kingdom and would be carried out as part of a multinational force. In 1956, political interference and the low state of military preparedness made the response too slow. The delay might have helped if the Egyptians were looking for a peaceful settlement, but this was made impossible by the British and French ultimatum and their collusion with Israel. As it was, logistics determined tactics, and it took months to bring forward the necessary craft and equipment, much of it from reserve, and then to carry out the essential training. When it became clear that the Egyptian Air Force had either been destroyed on the ground or had withdrawn, then a more flexible approach with calculated risk, leading to earlier paratroop landings and reinforcement, could have enabled the Allied forces to reach Suez and the southern end of the Canal and present the world with a *fait accompli*. Commanders on the spot made proposals to this end. The Amphibious Warfare Squadron, for example, was in a position to put troops ashore a day earlier than planned in order to take advantage of the successful parachute landings on 5 November.[25]

In the execution of the brief Suez campaign, great efforts were made to keep casualties to the minimum, especially among civilians. Wars cannot be fought without casualties, but it has recently been shown in actions in Europe and the Middle East that the public in Western countries find even the prospect of low casualties difficult to accept. On the other hand, the apparently constant images of dead and wounded on television news bulletins seem to inure them to such sights. Civilian casualties are particularly abhorred but not prevented. In 1956, while the British government was anxious to avoid civilian casualties, in doing so it was in danger of increasing the risk to its own troops. The restriction imposed on naval gunfire support to weapons below 6-inch could have prevented adequate supporting fire when the assault craft headed for the landing beaches of Port Said and Port Fouad. When the air strikes were ordered to attack only identified military vehicles, it was possible for the Egyptians to mix military and civilian traffic and make the task of the attacking aircraft nigh impossible under the rules of engagement imposed upon them. Refugees on the roads only made matters still worse.

It was a severe, some said 'exhilarating' test for the Admiralty to mount an amphibious operation in a defence strategy that contemplated global rather than limited war. When all was said and done, the Royal Navy, in close co-operation with the other services and the French, carried out what in many ways was a model operation, once it had been able to assemble the necessary forces. It was a success as far as it went. The immediately available resources were quickly deployed, while reserves in manpower and material were brought forward, albeit more slowly then the planners would have wished. The fact that the vessels required to carry out an assault landing took some time to bring to a satisfactory state of readiness was largely due to the low priority given to such operations in a nuclear age and a Cold War.

In summary, the Fleet Air Arm aircraft of the Carrier Group under Vice Admiral Power were quite outstanding, both in their effectiveness in attacking the Egyptian Air Force on the ground, and in the support they gave to the assault landings. The pioneering work of 845 Squadron and the Joint Helicopter Unit, flying from *Theseus* and *Ocean,* demonstrated the potential of the carrier borne helicopter in an assault role. They very much accelerated the notion of the Commando carrier and rapid response. The gunfire support given by the four destroyers that covered the sea landings was much appreciated by the Royal Marines Commandos. The landing craft pushed forward with determination to land their troops, tanks and other equipment. The 'Ton' class minesweepers, finding no mines in the northern approaches to the Canal, nevertheless gave confidence to the approaching landing craft, and later carried out essential patrol and communications tasks. The Replenishment Groups and the Royal Fleet Auxiliary effectively supported the various Task Groups; the operation could not have been mounted and sustained without them. When hostilities ended on 6 November, British salvage vessels, survey and clearance teams, bringing the accumulated experience of clearing wrecks after World War Two, were present and ready to clear the obstructions in the Canal.

Any study of *Operation Musketeer* cannot avoid drawing attention to the way in which events and attitudes in Britain affected the front line forces. Many of those engaged became resentful of the apparent lack of support from home. They could be wounded or killed, indeed some of them were, but those who heard about Hugh Gaitskell's broadcast were outraged, and others who took part have commented upon the muted response to their home-coming, described by one as 'coming home with our tails between our legs'. An angry sister, who had been opposed to the Suez venture throughout, confronted one Fleet Air Arm pilot on his return. Some of this resentment passed unnoticed by the servicemen engaged in the fighting until they reached home. They felt that they had been given a job to do and had done it well. Their frustration lay in having to stop before the job was properly finished. Politically the action against Egypt may have been misguided, but the performance of the three services had been commendable. The Fleet Air Arm personnel, though, felt particularly neglected when media reports attributed much of their efforts to the Royal Air Force.

There was redress in the statement in the House of Lords by the First Lord of the Admiralty, Viscount Hailsham, when he said in the debate on the Queen's speech on the opening of Parliament on 6 November:

> I am not sure how much it is realised that this was largely a naval operation. The aircraft were largely naval aircraft; the land forces were largely Marines, and, of course, the carriage was largely by sea. I know Your Lordships would desire me to say that that work was carried out with faultless efficiency and absolutely unswerving devotion to duty.[26]

Of course there may have been doubts among the men going to war about the justice of their cause. If so, their predicament was well described by Denis Healey MP for Leeds East, who had been involved in amphibious operations in World War Two and who was to become a future Secretary of State of Defence. He stated in the House of Commons on 3 November, before any landings had taken place:

> At this moment thousands of young Englishmen are sitting in landing craft moving from one destination in the Mediterranean towards the shores of Egypt. I spent some time in the last war in exactly that situation. While I was sitting in the landing craft waiting to fight against a known enemy, I did not have to worry my mind in the least about the honour of the cause I was defending.[27]

This view was largely reflected by the Army in identifying lessons to be learned from *Operation Musketeer*, an opinion no doubt felt by the other services:

> Lack of clear political aim and consistent political direction bedevilled the mounting and execution of the operation. Soldiers had no clear understanding of the reason for the operation and were thus deprived of any defence against hostile comment aimed at the operation from home or overseas.[28]

In a subsequent debate on the Navy Estimates, Mr Bottomley MP for Rochester and Chatham, did recognise what the services had achieved and also drew attention to some of the difficulties that had to be overcome. He said that Royal Navy personnel who served in the Suez fiasco had rendered magnificent service, carrying out their orders with great skill and efficiency. But administration and organisation had been 'thoroughly bad, stores and equipment which ought to have been ready on mobilisation had not been available, the loading of ships had been appalling and could have led to heavy loss of life if the enemy had been more formidable.'[29]

The last word by those in command of *Operation Musketeer* may be left to General Sir Charles Keightley, who concluded his report on the operation:

> Finally, in case the events which followed the Suez operations should have obscured the straight military success achieved I should like to record my admiration and gratitude to the sailors, soldiers and airmen who achieved all the military objectives given to them.

> The skill and gallantry required, particularly of parachutists, commandos and pilots was equal to that demanded in any operation of war and it is they more than anyone else who deserve praise.[30]

Even as these events occurred, developments were already taking place that would change naval warfare. Arguably the crisis of 1956 was the last occasion when a major operation was mounted using weaponry and tactics that were familiar in World War Two and the Korean War. The Royal Navy was well advanced in the design of its first nuclear submarine, HMS *Dreadnought*, and it was foreseen that the aircraft carrier and the nuclear submarine would form the spearhead of future naval power. The Seaslug ship to air missile had been under test since 1954 and the decision had been taken in 1955 that it would be fitted to the new 'County' class destroyers. Tests at sea of the new weapon were carried out from the guided weapons trials ship *Girdle Ness* during 1956-1958. The United States Navy had already adopted nuclear power for new aircraft carriers and submarines and guided missiles had been introduced in major warships and submarines in the form of the Regulus sub sonic cruise missile of limited range. The Soviet Navy sought to compete with the Western Powers, most notably in submarine warfare. In relatively quick time, more advanced missiles appeared, and they, with satellite navigation, communications and surveillance as well as computer controlled command systems dramatically changed the approach to naval warfare, whether it be global or limited.

Doctrine underlying the conduct of amphibious warfare was applied in 1956, with an amphibious operation recognised as a highly complex activity. Those involved in *Operation Musketeer* were committed at first to planning and carrying out an amphibious assault, and then, all too soon, to an amphibious withdrawal. The landings took place onto a hostile shore, even though on this occasion resistance was slight from the dug in tanks, guns and strong points facing the sea front in Port Said. The withdrawal was really unopposed but had to be conducted under spasmodic sniper fire and in a delicate political situation involving the United Nations. In addition to the large number of warships involved, no fewer than 90 ships of the Merchant Navy were requisitioned 'in connection with the Suez emergency'.[31] In the next major amphibious operation, in the Falklands in 1982, the same doctrine applied, but by then the control and operation of weaponry had changed, and functioned in a hi-tech environment. Unlike the Falklands campaign, the forces returning from Suez were not welcomed with crowds, bands, parades and honours. The whole venture was seen as a failure and a humiliation. The ship's company of the New Zealand cruiser *Royalist* had to wait until 2003 before a medal was struck commemorating the Suez campaign and thereby implicitly acknowledging that the ship had been directly involved. For the Royal Navy, as with the other services, no battle honours were forthcoming, instead a clasp 'Near East' was authorised as a bar to the General Service Medal. Awards to personnel were simply included in the New Year's Honour list.

Set in a global context, the chief lesson taught to the United Kingdom and France by the Suez affair was that imperial power, as they had understood it at least until 1939, was at an end. Power had shifted to the two superpowers and there was an emerging Third World of nations not aligned to either but beginning more forcefully to promote their own interests. Anthony Nutting, the Minister of State at the Foreign Office, entitled his account of the of government response to the crisis 'No End of a Lesson'. Although this quotation from Kipling, referring as it does to the Boer War, was contextually inappropriate, the phrase was apt. Yet all too often, lessons have to be learned again, and Suez was not to be the last time that the armed services would be called upon to play the role of fire engine in order to quench a conflagration lit by government policy

Appendix 1

Royal Navy Ships Engaged in Operations Musketeer and Toreador

Aircraft Carriers

Eagle	Captain H C D Maclean DSC RN
Albion	Captain R M Smeeton MBE RN
Bulwark	Captain J M Villiers OBE RN
Ocean	Captain I W T Beloe DSC RN
Theseus	Captain E F Pizey DSO RN

Cruisers

Jamaica	Captain A D Lenox-Conynham RN
Ceylon	Captain M E Butler-Bowdon OBE RN
Newfoundland	Captain J G Hamilton RN

Fast Minelayer

Manxman	Captain D S Tibbitts DSC RN

'Daring' class

Duchess	Captain N H G Austen DSO* RN
Defender	Captain M L Hardie DSC RN
Diamond	Captain M G Haworth DSC* RN
Decoy	Captain P J Hill-Norton RN
Diana	Captain J R Gower DSC RN
Daring	Captain D H R Bromley DSO RN

Destroyers

1st Destroyer Squadron

Chieftain	Captain A E T Christie OBE DSC** RN
Chaplet	Commander M F Renshaw RN
Chevron	Commander I D McLaughlan DSC* RN

3rd Destroyer Squadron

Armada	Captain A A F Talbot DSO* RN
St Kitts	Commander J A Murray OBE DSC RN
Barfleur	Commander L J Pearson RN

4th Destroyer Squadron

Alamein	Commander D V M MacLeod DSC RN

Frigates

6th Frigate Squadron

Undine	Captain J F D Bush DSC** RN
Ursa	Commander A M Power MBE RN
Ulysses	Commander G H Peters RN
Urania	Commander G R Callingham RN

3rd Frigate Squadron

Crane	Captain B S Pemberton RN
Modeste	Commander C E C Dickens RN

Headquarters and Maintenance Ships

Tyne	Captain J W H Bennett DSC RN
Meon	Commodore R de L Brooke DSO DSC* RN
Forth	Captain V J H Van der Byl DSC RN & Cdr the Hon T V Stopford RN
Woodbridge Haven	Captain J H Walwyn OBE RN
Ranpura	Captain N H Pond RN

Submarines

Tudor	Lt Commander W G Edwards RN

Landing Ships Tank

Striker	Commander H H Dannreuther RN
Puncher	Commander I Hall DSC RN
Suvla	Commander R A Gilchrist RN
Reggio	Lt Commander I M Stoop DSC RN
Ravager	Lt Commander R Johnston DSC RN
Anzio	Lt Commander B D Davidson RN
Lofoten	Lt Commander P F C Coulson-Davis RN
Salerno	Lt Commander J S Pallot RN

Landing Craft Tank

Parapet	Lt Commander E A Hawksworth DSC RN
Portcullis	Lt Commander K Alan-Williams RN
Bastion	Lt Commander A H L Harvey DSC RN
Rampart	Lt Commander L Lamb DSM RN
Citadel	Lt Commander J A H Langton RN
Redoubt	Lt Commander J C Waters RN
Counterguard	Lieutenant C M G Bankart RN
Buttress	Lieutenant P F Trevorah RN
Sallyport	Lieutenant I B Lennox RN

Survey Ship

Dalrymple	Lt Commander J D Winstanley RN

Minesweepers

In the Naval Report on *Operation Musketeer* it is stated that 15 Coastal Minesweepers took part in the operations but they are not named. They were probably:

104 M/S Squadron	**105 M/S Squadron**	**108 M/S Squadron**
Alcaston(SO)	*Appleton(SO)*	*Sefton(SO)*
Coniston	*Blaxton*	*Dufton*
Darlaston	*Edderton*	*Fenton*
Letterston	*Upton*	*Hickleton*
		Kildarton
		Leverton
		Shavington

Royal Fleet Auxiliary

24 Replenishment and Supply ships are listed:

Tiderace	*Tiderange*	*Tidereach*
Eddybeach	*Olna*	*Retainer*
Wave Sovereign	*Wave Laird*	*Wave Conqueror*
Wave Master	*Wave Victor*	*Wave Protector*
Brown Ranger	*Blue Ranger*	*Fort Sandusky*
Fort Duquesne	*Fort Charlotte*	*Fort Dunvegan*
Amherst	*Eaglesdale*	*Echodale*
Spaburn	*Spapool*	*Surf Pioneer*

Fleet Air Arm Squadrons.

800 (Sea Hawks)	Lt Commander J D Russell RN
802 (Sea Hawks)	Lt Commander R L Eveleigh RN
804 (Sea Hawks)	Lt Commander R von T B Kettle RN
809 (Sea Venoms)	Lt Commander R A Shilcock RN
810 (Sea Hawks)	Lt Commander P M Lamb DSC AFC RN
830 (Wyverns)	Lt Commander C V Howard RN
892 (Sea Venoms)	Lt Commander M J H Petrie RN

Appendix 2

Fleet Air Arm Aircraft engaged in Operation Musketeer

De Havilland Sea Venom   Night and all weather fighter, crew of 2

Armament: Four 20 mm cannon, underwing provision for two 500 lb
            bombs or eight 60 lb rockets
Speed: 537 knots
Range: 705 miles

Douglas Skyraider   Airborne early warnings aircraft, crew of 3

Armament: None
Speed: 305 knots
Range: max 3000 miles

Hawker Sea Hawk   Single seater fighter, fighter-bomber or
                           ground attack aircraft

Armament: Four 20 mm cannon; provision for ten 3inch rockets or up to
            four 500 lb bombs
Speed: 520 knots
Range: 288 miles

Westland Wyvern   Single seater torpedo strike fighter

Armament: Four 20mm cannon in wings, provision for one torpedo,
            three 1000 lb or 500 lb bombs, or eight 3-inch or sixteen
            2-inch rockets
Speed: 330 knots
Range: 904 miles

EGYPTIAN AIR FORCE

The chief threat to the Fleet came from Russian built aircraft

Mikoyan-Gurevich MiG-15   Single seat fighter

    Armament: Standard armament - two 23 mm cannon and one 37 mm
                    cannon below nose, provision for rockets or two 1000 lb
                    bombs
    Speed: 670 mph

Ilyushin Il-28   Twin jet light attack bomber

    Armament: Two fixed forward firing 23 mm cannon; two 23 mm
                    cannon in tail turret
    Speed: 580 mph
    Range: c 1500 miles

Appendix 3

Wrecks in Port Said Harbour

No	Type	Type	Tonnage	Date Removed
1	*No 823*	150 ton crane	1700	completed 21.1.57
2	*No 827*	80 ton crane	1300	surveyed
3.	*No 839*	15 ton crane	365	30.11.56
4.	*Pollux*	salvage craft	1500	no work done
5	*Peleuse*	bucket dredger	2900	no work done
6	*Paul Solente*	suction dredger	4000	16.1.57
7	*Neptune*	hopper	1500	15.12.56
8	*Triton*	hopper	1500	24.11.56
9		floating dock	2700	10.12.56
9a	*Bassel*	tug	400	6.12.56
10	*No 37*	hopper	1450	13.12.56
11	*Iacovos*	merchant ship	2500	no work done
12	*No 44*	hopper	1000	6.12.56
13	*No 6*	dredger	1200	no work done

No	Type	Type	Tonnage	Date Removed
14	*No 19*	bucket dredger	1900	wires passed
15	*Ardent*	tug	190	2.1.57
16	*Agile*	tug	190	6.1.57
	Cheddid	tug	280	
	Quircg	tug	280	4.1.57
17	*Hercule*	tug	1200	11.1.57
18	*Le Hardi*	pilot boat	490	17.12.56
19	*Garii*	tug	235	7.12.56
19a	*Barq*	tug	350	3.12.56
20	*Actif*	tug	115	no work done

Appendix 4

Merchant Ships Requisitioned during the Period of Operation Musketeer and Aftermath

In any substantial combined operation on the scale of *Operation Musketeer*, the Royal Navy must fulfil its traditional role of facilitating the successful landing of the Army on a potentially hostile shore and then keeping it supplied. At the same time it must not only provide covering fire from supporting warships but also, in an age of carrier borne aviation, provide substantial air support to the Army ashore. Air cover would also protect the Fleet against enemy air attack. However, if the maritime force was to have the strength to mount and then sustain an operation, it must depend heavily upon the Merchant Navy. Personnel, equipment, ammunition, fuel, water and stores of all kinds must be brought to the scene of operations. In 1956, Britain still maintained a large merchant fleet and was able, in an emergency, to call upon British ships to support military operations. Many such ships were requisitioned as early as August 1956, shortly after the crisis first developed and were held until after the *Operation Musketeer* was over. They bear testimony to the contribution made by British owned companies. Some ships were retained until the final withdrawal and were not released until early in 1957.

This is not a complete list of merchant vessels requisitioned during the whole of the Suez Crisis, but only of those in service during the period from October 1956 up to January 1957.

Name	Owner	Date of Requisition	Date of Release
mv Ambassador	Hall Bros SS Co	14.8.56	7.12.56
mv Amber	Wm Robertson	15.8.56	28.12.56
ss Avistone	Aviation & Shipping Co	8.8.56	5.12.56

Name	Owner	Date of Requisition	Date of Release
mv Baltic Clipper	United Baltic Corp	14.8.56	17.12.56
mv Beechmore	Johnston Warren Lines	21.8.56	30.11.56
mv Beihan	Aden Shipping Co	8.11.56	3.1.57
ss Bellerby	Ropner Shipping Co	31.8.56	5.12.56
ss Benin Palm	Palm Line	23.8.56	12.12.56
ss Benledi	Wm Thomson & Co	6.8.56	29.11.56
mv Benvannock	Ben Line	22.8.56	23.11.56
ss Borde	Stephenson Clarke Ltd	8.11.56	9.1 57
ss Brookhurst	Rex Shipping Co Ltd	11.8.56	7.12.56
mv Cardiff Brook	Williamstown Shipping	17.8.56	9.1 57
ss Cedarpool	Pool Shipping Co	14.8.56	7.12.56
ss Chandler	Elder Dempster (Canada)	11.8.56	7.12.56
mv Cornish City	Reardon Smith Line	14.8.56	23.11.56
mv Cressington Court	Court Line Ltd	10.8.56	23.11.56
ss Curran	Shamrock Shipping Co	17.8.56	16.11.56
mv Daleby	Ropner Shipping Co	5.11.56	8.1.57
ss Eastern Glory	Indo-China Steam Nav Co	1.11.56	19.11.56
mv Egidia	Anchor Line Ltd	10.8.56	28.12.56
mv El Hak	Halal Shipping Co	5.10.56	28.12.56
mv England	Currie Line Ltd	17.8.56	16.11.56
ss Garlinge	Constants Ltd	17.8.56	29.11.56
mv Georgina Everard	F T Everard & Sons	7.8.56	23.11.56
ss Glenshiel	Glen Line Ltd	15.8.56	7.12.56

Name	Owner	Date of Requisition	Date of Release
ss *Gogovale*	Buchanan Shipping Co	3.8.56	13.11.56
ss *Granny Suzanne*	Trafalgar Steamship Co	10.8.56	19.11 56
ss *Harpagon*	J & C Harrison Ltd	17.8.56	12.12.56
mv *Hartismere*	National Steamship Co	3.8.56	5.12.56
mv *Huntsland*	Power Steamship Co Ltd	14.8.56	19.11.56
mv *Kenilworth Castle*	Union Castle Mail SS Co	15.8.56	27.11.56
ss *Kingsbury*	Alexander Shipping Co	10.8.56	7.12.56
mv *La Ensenada*	Buries Markes Ltd	15.8.56	5.12.56
mv *Lepton*	Shell Petroleum Co Ltd	1.11.56	21.11.56
ss *Loch Maddy*	SS 'Mombasa' Co Ltd	15.8.56	10.12.56
ss *Marshall*	'K' Steamship Co Ltd	10.8.56	10.12 56
ss *Midhurst*	Rex Shipping Co Ltd	11.8.56	7.12.56
ss *Mountpark*	Denholm Line Steamers Ltd	14.8.56	15.11.56
ss *North Britain*	North Shipping Co Ltd	20.8.56	7.12.56
mv *Paraguay*	Royal Mail Lines Ltd	10.8.56	10.12.56
mv *Parkgate*	Turnbull Scott Shipping Co	14.8.56	7.12.56
ss *Prospector*	Charente Steamship Co Ltd	9.8.56	7.12.56
ss *Rivercrest*	Ivanovic & Co Ltd	7.8.56	7.12.56
ss *Romilly*	Aden Coal Co Ltd (Aden)	13.11.56	3.1.57
mv *Salinas*	Pacific Steam Nav Co Ltd	15.8.56	16.11.56
ss *Sandsend*	Rowland & Marwood's Co	.8.56	5.12.56
mv *Scottish Trader*	Trader Navigation Co Ltd	3.8.56	5.12.56
ss *Seaboard Enterprise*	Seabord Owners Ltd(Canada)	15.8.56	23.11.56

Name	Owner	Date of Requisition	Date of Release
mv Seiyun	Aden Shipping Co	8.11.56	3.1.57
mv Shibam	Aden Shipping Co	8.11.56	3.1.57
ss Sunkirk	John Kilgour Co Ltd	7.8.56	28.12.56
mv Temple Hall	Temple Steamship Co Ltd	13.8.56	27.11.56
ss Tregenna	Hain Steamship Co Ltd	7.8.56	12.12.56
ss Tregothnan	Hain Steamship Co Ltd	22.8.56	12.12.56
mv Windsor	Britain Steamship Co Ltd	14.8.56	20.11.56

Troopships

Ascania	1925	14013 tons	
Asturias	1925	22445 tons	
Dilwara	1936	12555 tons	
Dunera	1937	12615 tons	
Empire Fowey	1935	19121 tons	ex German *Potsdam*
Empire Ken	1928	9523 tons	ex German *Ubena*
Empire Parkeston	1930	5576 tons	ex *Port Henry*
New Australia	1938	36667	

Chartered Transport Ferries (ex LST) (known as Bustard boats).

Empire Doric	*Empire Gaelic*	*Empire Celtic*
Empire Baltic	*Empire Cedric*	*Empire Cymric*
Empire Nordic		

Appendix 5

Naval Staff, Operation Musketeer

Captain C P Mills DSC — SCO (Chief Staff Officer)
Cdr A T Rees/ Cdr I R Humphrey — Secretaries
Cdr A D Bulman — SGO (Gunnery)
Cdr M F Fell DSO DSC — SO (Air)
Cdr E F Gueritz DSC — SO(Q)(Logistics).
Cdr A D Casswell — SO(P) (Plans)
Lt Cdr R Durnford — SCO (Communications)
Lt Cdr W J Woolley — SNO (Navigation)
Lt Cdr W E B Godsal — STASO (Torpedo, Anti- Submarine & Mine Warfare)
Lt Cdr J T Crawley — SOO (Operations)
Lt Cdr A Wylie — SGO2
Lt A A Browne — SCO2 (& Flag Lt to Vice Admiral Richmond)
Lt P N Marsden — Sec/SCO
CCO E W A Collins — SCO3
Lt Col W A T Gethin RA — NGSCLO (Gunfire Support Liaison)
Major J T O Waters RM/ — SO(W)
Major D P L Hunter RM
Captain A M Robertson RM — SO(I) (Intelligence)

(List drawn from Vice-Admiral Richmond's Report on *Operation Musketeer* - TNA ADM 116 6209)

The nucleus of the maritime element of the staff responsible for planning *Operation Musketeer* was formed from the staff of FO2 Mediterranean, at first Vice Admiral Richmond, and then Vice Admiral Durnford Slater. Planning began in London, but in due course the staff moved to Malta and Cyprus.

The aircraft carrying Admiral Sir Guy Grantham, his Flag Lt, Lt D H Morse, Lt Cdr W E B Godsal and Lt P N Marsden to Cyprus also had on board a large number of brown envelopes containing the operational order for *Musketeer*. Due to the pilot being 'not too happy with the starboard engine', the aircraft diverted to land at El Adem in Libya, a state not supportive of British policy towards Egypt. If forced to remain on the ground for too long, the aircraft could be held by the Libyan authorities. Despite some scares as Libyan security staff boarded the aircraft, repairs were completed, the aircraft continued to Cyprus with its secret documents intact and a very awkward situation was avoided.

(Correspondence Rear Admiral Marsden 4 November 2004 and Captain W E B Godsal 6 January 2005)

Bibliography

Ambrose S E	Eisenhower: Soldier and President	New York 1990
Baer G W	One Hundred Years of Sea Power	Stanford 1994
Bamberger M&S	Secrets of Suez	London 1957
Barker A J	Suez; the Seven Day War	London 1964
Barnett C	The Verdict of Pace	London 2001
Beaufre A	The Suez Expedition 1956	London 1969
Brooke A J	Photo Reconnaissance	London 1975
Cull B et al	Wings over Suez	London 1996
Dockrill M	British Defence Since 1945	Oxford 1988
Doust M J	Phantom Leader	Suffolk 2005
Fell Capt W R	The Sea Surrenders	London 1960
Fergusson B	Water Maze-the Story of Combined Operations	London 1961
Friedman N	Seapower and Space	London 2000
Fullick R & Powell G	Suez: the Double War	London 1979
Grove E	Vanguard to Trident	London 1987
Habesch D	The Army's Navy	London 2001
Healey D	The Time of My Life	London 1989
Hennessy P	The Prime Minister	London 2000
Herzog C	The Arab-Israeli Wars	London 1982
Hill Rear Adm J R	Maritime Strategy for Medium Powers	London 1986
	Lewin of Greenwich	London 2000

Hobbs Cdr D	Aircraft of the Royal Navy Since 1945	Liskeard 1983
Hobbs Cdr D	Aircraft Carriers of the Royal and Commonwealth Navies	London 1996
Jackson Gen Sir W & Bramall Field Marshal Lord	The Chiefs	London 1992
Kemp P J	The T-class Submarine	London 1990
Kent Captain B	Signal	Clanfield, Hampshire 1993
Kyle K	Suez	London 1991
Ladd J A	By Sea, By Land	London 1998
Lee ACM Sir D	Wings in the Sun	London 1989
Love R W (Ed)	The Chiefs of Naval Operations	Annapolis
Marriott L	Royal Navy Destroyers Since 1945	London 1989
Mills Cdr D F	It Is Upon The Navy	Hereford 1994
Milne Lt Cdr J M	Flashing Blades over the Sea	Liskeard (nd)
Mitchell W H & Sawyer L A	The Empire Ships	London 1990
Mosley L	Dulles	London 1978
Murfett M H (Ed)	The First Sea Lords (Fisher to Mountbatten)	Westport 1995
Neff D	Warriors at Suez	New York 1981
Nott J	Here Today Gone Tomorrow	London 2002
Nutting A Roskill S London 1976	No End of a Lesson Naval Policy Between the Wars 1930-1939	London 1967
Sowdon D	Admiralty Coastal Salvage Vessels	Windsor 2005

Speller I	The Role of Amphibious Warfare in British Defence Policy, 1945-1956	Basingstoke 2001
Sturtivant R & Ballance T	The Squadrons of the Fleet Air Arm	Tonbridge 1994
Sturtivant R, Burrows M & Howard L	Fleet Air Arm Fixed Wing Aircraft Since 1946	Tonbridge 2004
Thomas H	The Suez Affair	London 1967
Varble D	The Suez Crisis 1956	Oxford 2003
Wettern D	The Decline of British Sea Power	London 1982
Ziegler P	Mountbatten; the Official Biography	London 1985

Journals.

Air Enthusiast No 74, March/April 1998: J T Smith *Wrath of a Mythical Monster.*

Air Pictorial August/September 1968: V Flintham, The Suez Campaign 1956.

Flight Deck   *HMS Ocean and HMS Theseus*
Life in the Old Dogs Yet, Lt Cdr J C Jacob RN Autumn 1956
HMS Albion   Winter 1956
HMS Albion in the Mediterranean   Spring 1957
HMS Bulwark
HMS Eagle

Naval Review Vol XLV No 1 January 1957   Oscar', *The Seaborne Assault on Port Said.*
No 2 April 1957   J S, *The Aircraft Carrier Aspects of Musketeer.*
The Amphibious Assault on Port Said.

US Naval War College Review, March 1969, Rear Admiral H E Eccles USN, *Suez 1956, Some Military Lessons.* March 1970, Lt Cdr W B Garrett USN, *The US Navy's Role in the 1956 Suez Crisis.*

US Naval Institute Proceedings Vol 90, No 4, April 1964, Lt Cdr J Stewart RN, *The Suez Operation.*

References

FAAM The Fleet Air Arm Museum, Yeovilton, Somerset.
IWM   Imperial War Museum
MAF   The Museum of Army Flying, Middle Wallop, Wilts.
NHB   Naval Historical Branch, Portsmouth.
RMM   The Royal Marines Museum
TM   Tank Museum, Bovingdon.
TNA   The National Archives, Kew.

Chapter 1   The Political Background.

1.   Kyle K, *Suez* p 136.
2.   Ibid p 329.
3.   Hennessy P, *The Prime Ministers* Ch 9 p 217, and Ambrose S, *Eisenhower, Soldier and Statesman* Ch 17 pp 415-433.
4.   TNA DEFE 4 82, Chiefs of Staff, 26 January 1957: cf Kyle p 92.
5.   Jackson & Bramall, *The Chiefs* pp 299-301.

Chapter 2   Planning and Assembling the Forces

1.   NHB, Naval Operations Orders, Commander TF 345, 27 October 1956.
2.   Beaufre, General A, *The Suez Expedition 1956*, p 28.
3.   Ibid p 269.
4.   Wettern D, *The Decline of British Seapower*, p 133.
5.   NHB, Naval Operations Orders, Commander TF 345, 27 October 1956.
6.   TNA CAB 134 1216, Minutes of Egypt Committee 2 August 1956.
7.   FAAM, Pink List July - December 1956
8.   TNA ADM 1 26826, Manpower Problems, CinC Home Fleet to CinC Portsmouth, 10 October 1956.
9.   TNA ADM 1 27373, The Planning Stage, Director of Welfare and Service Conditions.

10. NHB Vol 52B, Reports of Proceedings; TNA
    ADM 1 27373 sects 212-216.
11. Vice-Admiral Sir Charles Mills, correspondence with author,
    July 2005.
12. Rear-Admiral E R Gueritz, interview with author, July 2005.
13. TNA ADM 116 6135, Operation Musketeer, Supply and
    Manpower.
14. Rear-Admiral Gueritz interview.
15. TNA DEFE 5 70, The Future Role of the Navy, July 1956.
16. Speller I, *Amphibious Operations 1945-1998* in
    Harding R (Ed) *The Royal Navy 1930-2000 Innovation
    and Defence.*
17. TNA ADM 1 26666, Logistic Support and Administrative
    Planning.
18. Lt Cdr J Pallot RN, e-mail November 2004.
19. TNA WO 288 75, 3rd Infantry Division War Diary.
20. TNA DEFE 2 2056, Amphibious Loading of LST at
    Plymouth, August/ September 1956.
21. TM, Major J B Joly, Narrative.
22. TNA ADM 116 6136, Report of Proceedings, Amphibious
    Warfare Squadron.
23. Ibid.
24. Ibid, sect 364-367.
25. TNA WO 288 60, Availability of ex RN LST Out of
    Reserve.
26. '*Times of Malta*', 28 November 1956.
27. Habesch D *The Army's Navy* pp 138-142.
28. TNA MT 40 187, Lessons Learned from the Suez Crisis,
    Requisition Order, 3 August 1956.
29. TNA WO 106 5986, Operation Musketeer, Military Planning.
30. Ibid.
31. Lee, Air Marshal Sir David, *Wings in the Sun*, pp 68-71.
32. Jackson & Bramall, *The Chiefs* p 299.

Chapter 3   The Carriers Strike.

1. TNA ADM 116 6097, Anglo-French Intervention in Suez Canal
   Dispute; CinC Mediterranean to Admiralty 28 July 1956.
2. TNA ADM 116 6104, Flag Officer Aircraft Carriers, Report of
   Proceedings.
3. TNA ADM 116 6103, Operation Musketeer, Operation
   Toreador Reports of Proceedings TF 324.
4. TNA ADM 219 610, Aircraft Armament Loads.
5. FAAM, Howard J W, Midshipman's Log.
6. TNA ADM 116 6104, FOAC Report of Proceedings.

7.   TNA ADM 116 6097, Anglo-French Intervention in Suez Canal Dispute. (This file contains much correspondence on the *Royalist* issue, with additional signals on 1 and 4 November).
8.   TNA ADM 53 143221, log HMS *Albion*, 2 November 1956.
9.   TNA AIR 20 10746 Report of Proceedings Flag Officer Aircraft Carriers, sect 12.
10.   Parliamentary Debates, Vol 560 col 925, 14 November 1956.
11.   FAAM, RAE Farnborough, *Trials of BH5 Type Catapults for HMS Eagle* 1952.
12.   TNA ADM 205 139, CinC Mediterranean to Admiralty.
13.   TNA ADM 116 6104, FOAC, Report of Proceedings.
14.   NHB Operation Musketeer, Naval Operations Orders.
15.   TNA ADM 116 6117, Admiral Task Force to FOAC, 28 October 1956.
16.   TNA ADM 116 6104, FOAC Report of Proceedings.
17.   IWM 96/10/2, Air Marshal (Sir) Denis Barnett, Report on Operation Musketeer.
18.   NHB Naval Operations Orders, CO TF 345 27 October 1956
19.   TNA ADM 116 6209, Diary of Events.
20.   TNA AIR 8 1940, General Sir Charles Keightley, Despatch, Operations in Egypt November-December 1956, *The London Gazette* 10 September 1956.
21.   TNA AIR 20 10746. FOAC Summary of Operations.
22.   Brooke A J, *Photo Reconnaissance* p 224.
23.   Lee Air Chief Marshal Sir David, *Wings in the Sun*, Ch 6.
24.   (Lt) P. Cardew RN, e-mail 31 May 2005.
25.   FAAM, Squadrons Record Books.
26.   Bussey G, *Westland Wyvern*, Jabberwock No 39, Spring 1998.
27.   TNA ADM 53 142865, log HMS *Albion*, November 1956.
28.   FAAM, 899 Squadron Records.
29.   FAAM, *Flight Deck*, Winter 1956, HMS *Albion*, (Reports on the activities of the aircraft carriers in Operation Musketeer appear in this edition).
30.   FAAM, Suez File, HMS *Eagle*, Air Operations.
31.   TNA ADM 53 143861 log HMS *Eagle*, November 1956.
32.   IWM 96/10/2 Air Marshal Denis Barnett, Report on Operation Musketeer, p 3(e).
33.   TNA AIR 20 10746, FOAC Report of Proceedings.
34.   Ibid.
35.   'Fly One' refers to a location far forward on the flight deck, to the side of the angled deck, where aircraft may park after landing.
36.   AIR 8 1940, General Keightley Despatch.
37.   FAAM, Suez File, HMS *Eagle*, Air Operations.
38.   Mills Cdr D, *It is upon The Navy* Ch 14.
39.   FAAM, 814 Squadron Record Book.
40.   FAAM, 899 Squadron Record Book, 6 November 1956.

41.   FAAM, Suez File, HMS *Eagle* Air Operations; website http//britains-smallwars.co.suez.
42.   TNA ADM 202 455, 3 Commando Brigade Report.
43.   Whittaker T W, http://britains-smallwars.co.suez/ground-liaison.
44.   TNA ADM 116 6209, Naval Report, Diary p 172.
45.   FAAM, J W Howard, Midshipman's log, HMS *Eagle*.
46.   TNA AIR 20 10746, FOAC Summary of Operations During Operation Musketeer sec 55.
47.   ADM 173 2459, HMS *Tudor* engine room log, 27 October-9 November 1956.
48.   ADM 116 6104, Reports of Proceedings HMS *Tudor*.
49.   ADM 116 6119, FOAC to SM1, 4 November 1956.
50.   Kemp P J, *The T Class Submarine*, pp 128-129.
51.   Kent, Captain B RN, *Signal*, p 188 refers to Rugby's VLF shore to submarine transmissions.
52.   Information on *Tudor*'s patrol comes from Lt T J Andrews RN e-mail, November 2004 and ERA R McKenzie, e-mail September 2004.
53.   IWM 96/10/2, Air Marshal Barnett Report.
54.   TNA ADM 116 6104, FOAC Report.
55.   FAAM, Report, 63 CBGL Section HMS *Eagle*.
56.   TNA AIR 20 10746, FOAC Summary, sect 59.
57.   The Mountbatten memo is at the end of ADM 116 6104.

Chapter 4   *Ocean* **and** *Theseus*, **The Helicopter Landings.**

1.   TNA ADM 1 27051, Operation Musketeer Carrier Operations, Appendix 5, *The Use of Helicopters to Lift 45 Commando Royal Marines*; FAAM Jacob, *Life in the Old Dogs Yet, Flight Deck*, Autumn 1956.
2.   DEFE 2 1604, *Conversion of Carrier Hulls for use as Combined Operations Assault Ships*.
3.   *Jane's Fighting Ships*, 1957-58.
4.   FAAM, 705 Squadron Records.
5.   TNA ADM 1 27051, Operation Musketeer, Carrier Operations.
6.   Ibid sect 5.
7.   FAAM 845 Squadron Diary.
8.   TNA ADM 1 26450 *Mass Helicopter Trials*, 24 October 1956.
9.   Ibid .
10.   Ibid .
11.   MAF, Office of CTG 345.9 HMS *Ocean*, Joint Operation Order No. 2 sect, 2,3.
12.   IWM P 68, Sayer, Rear Admiral G B, Home Fleet Training Squadron, Report of Proceedings 23 November 1956.

13. FAAM Suez File, HMS *Ocean*, Commander's Daily Orders, 5-6 November 1956.
14. MAF, Graham Bell, Major F, *The Other Side of the Coin*.
15. MAF, Joint Helicopter Unit (JHU) War Diary, August-November 1956.
16. IWM PP/MCR/355 Ashton A R, Papers.
17. IWM P 68 Rear Admiral G B Sayer, Home Fleet Training Squadron, Report of Proceedings.
18. MAF, JHU *An Outline History of the Joint Experimental Helicopter Unit*.
19. Correspondence, Rear Admiral Gueritz, July 2005.
20. Ibid.

Chapter 5 **Assault from the Sea.**

1. TNA AIR 8 1940, General Keightley Despatch.
2. Ibid.
3. http//www.britains-smallwars.co.suez/communications.
4. IWM 96/10/3, Air Marshal D Barnett, Report on Operation Musketeer, sect 28.
5. Weston R, Midshipman's log, HMS *Bastion*.
6. TNA ADM 116 6136, CinC Mediterranean Naval Report, Amphibious Warfare Squadron correspondence.
7. Ibid, sect 372.
8. Weston R, interview with author, December 2004.
9. Lt Cdr J Pallot RN, e-mail December 2004.
10. TNA ADM 116 6102, Office of Flag Officer Flotillas, Report of Proceedings sect 5, 18 November 1956.
11. TNA ADM 116 6136, CinC Mediterranean Report, sect 372/373.
12. TNA ADM 116 6102, Vice-Admiral Durnford-Slater, Report of Proceedings, sect 10.
13. Ibid, sect 10, 11.
14. Ibid sect 74.
15. Ibid sect 15.
16. Ibid sect 16.
17. NHB, Naval Operations Orders, 'Intelligence'.
18. NHB, Commodore R de L Brooke, AWS Report of Proceedings.
19. NHB, Naval Operation Orders TF 345, 27 October 1956.
20. TNA ADM 116 6102, Naval Officer-in-Charge, Report of Proceedings, sect 8, 21 November 1956.
21. '*Times of Malta*', 29 December 1956.
22. NHB, Naval Operation Orders, TF 345 27 October 1956.
23. TNA ADM 116 6136, Amphibious Warfare Squadron Report.
24. TNA ADM 53 143697, log HMS *Decoy*, November 1956.

25.   NHB Operation Musketeer, Vol 52B
26.   TNA ADM 53 143362, log HMS *Chaplet*, November 1956.
27.   'Times of Malta', 28 November 1956.
28.   TNA ADM 116 6136, AWS Report, sect 377
29.   NHB, Commodore, Amphibious Warfare Squadron Report.
30.   TM, 6th Royal Tank Regiment War Diary: cf WO 288 161.
31.   TNA WO 288 161, 6th Royal Tank Regiment War Diary, November 1956.
32.   TNA WO 288 160, 161, War Diary.
33.   NHB, Commodore R de L Brooke, Report of Proceedings.
34.   TNA ADM 53 144844, log HMS *Portcullis*, November 1956
35.   'Peregrine', *The Amphibious Assault on Port Said*, Naval Review Vol XLV No 2, April 1957.
36.   Ibid.
37.   TNA ADM 116 6102, Report Naval Officer in Charge, Port Said.
38.   TNA AIR 8 1940, General Keightley Despatch.
39.   Interview, Captain M Fulford-Dobson RN, April 2005.
40.   Beaufre, General A, *The Suez Expedition*, pp 111-115.
41.   Kyle K, *Suez* pp 474-477.
42.   Interview Captain Fulford Dobson RN.
43.   TNA WO 288 128, 1st Btn Royal Scots War Diary.
44.   TNA WO 288 129, 1st Btn Argyll & Sutherland Highlanders War Diary.
45.   TNA AIR 20 1940 General Keightley Despatch, p 5336.

Chapter 6   **Operation Toreador.**

1.   TNA ADM 116 6209, Vice Admiral M Richmond, Naval Report on Operation Musketeer.
2.   TNA ADM 116 6103, Captain J G Hamilton RN, Report of Proceedings, HMS *Newfoundland*: cf IWM 94/32/1 Capt J R Gower DSC RN, An Illustrated Memoir, Reports of Proceedings..
3.   IWM 94/32/1 Captain J R Gower.
4.   TNA ADM 116 6209.
5.   IWM 94/32/1, Captain J R Gower, Illustrated Memoir.
6.   TNA ADM 6118, CTF 324 to CinC Mediterranean, 1 November 1956.
7.   TNA ADM 116 6138 contains a folder with plots of this action.
8.   Correspondence PO H O'Grady (later Lt Com OBE), Narrative of Events, HMS *Crane*)
9.   TNA ADM 116 6105, Reports of Proceedings CTF 324, 18 November 1956.
10.   ibid, '*Crane* sails to pay off'.

11.   TNA ADM 116 6209, Vice Admiral M Richmond, Naval Report

Chapter 7   The United States Sixth Fleet.

1.   Love R (ed), *The Chiefs of Naval Operations* p 283.
2.   TNA ADM 116 6118, Signal 1 November 1956.
3.   Ibid.
4.   TNA ADM 116 6138, COS Meetings, 1 & 2 November 1956
5.   TNA ADM 116 6209, 30 October 1956.
6.   TNA ADM 116 6118, CTF to Adm 31 October 1956.
7.   Ibid, signal, CTG 1 November 1956.
8.   Garrett Lt Cdr W B, *US Navy's Role in the 1956 Suez Crisis*, US Naval College Review, March 1970, pp 66-78.
9.   TNA ADM 116 6118, CinC Mediterranean to ComSixthfleet.
10.   TNA ADM 116 6136, Naval Reports, CinC Mediterranean
11.   Ibid.
12.   Garrett, Lt Cdr W B USN, *US Navy's Role in the 1956 Suez Crisis*, Naval War College Review March 1970 pp 66-78.
13.   TNA ADM 116 6118, HMS *Ulysses* to USS *Macon*, 2 November 1956
14.   TNA ADM 53 143221, log HMS *Bulwark*, 4 November 1956.
15.   TNA ADM 116 6136, Naval Reports, CinC Mediterranean.
16.   TNA ADM 116 6119 CTG 345 to CinC Mediterranean.
17.   TNA AIR 20 10746, Flag Officer Aircraft Carriers Report, sect 18.
18.   TNA AIR 8 1940, General Keightley Despatch.

Chapter 8   Cease Fire, Withdrawal and Clearing the Canal.

1.   TNA AIR 8 1940, General Keightley Despatch, p 5336 sect 10.
2.   Ibid, sect 10.
3.   Ibid sect 10.
4.   TNA ADM 116 6102, Naval Officer in Command, Report of Proceedings sect 10.
5.   E-mail, John Hard (HMS *Forth*) July 2004; Fell Captain W R, *The Sea Surrenders*, p 160.
6.   TNA ADM 116 6109, Anglo-French Intervention in Suez Canal Dispute; Captain Podger RN, Report of Proceedings, 1 February 1957.
7.   Cdr A Browne RN, narrative September 2005.
8.   FAAM, 849 Sqdn, 'A' Flight Diary.
9.   FAAM 899 Sqdn Diary.
10.   FAAM 849 Sqdn, 'A' Flight Diary.

11. Habesch D, *The Army's Navy* p 140.
12. E-mail Lt Cdr J Pallot RN, 16 November 2004.
13. TNA ADM 116 6105, Vice- Admiral Durnford-Slater Report of Proceedings 31 December 1956.
14. ADM 116 6105, Naval Task Force Commander, Appendix D, Narrative of Events 11 November 1956.
15. Ibid.
16. TNA WO 288 55, Final Phase of Embarkation.
17. FAAM 849 Sqdn, 'A' Flight, 23/24 December 1956.
18. TNA AIR 8 1940, General Keightley Despatch.
19. Parliamentary Papers 1956/1957, Vol 560 col 76, 6 November 1956.
20. TNA ADM 53 143622 log HMS *Chevron*, November 1956.
21. Fell, Captain W R, *The Sea Surrenders* p 196.
22. Naval Review, Vol XLV No 1, January 1957, Naval Affairs pp 70-73, Salvage Operations.
23. TNA ADM 116 6108, Wrecks at Port Said are listed.
24. Fell, Captain W R, pp 161-163.
25. TNA ADM 116 6209: ADM 53 143839, log HMS *Dufton*, November 1956: ADM 53 145137, log HMS *Sefton*, November 1956.
26. TNA ADM 116 6109, Report of Proceedings, 1 February 1956, sect 4.
27. TNA ADM 116 6138, undated note.
28. TNA ADM 116 6109, Captain Podger's Report of Proceedings, 1 February 1957.
29. FAAM, Ship's Folder HMCS *Magnificent*, p 55.
30. Ibid.
31. Letter to the author, 26 January 2005.
32. Fell, Captain W R, p 230.
33. Doust, M J, *Phantom Leader*, pp 181-182.

Chapter 9   **An Overview.**

1. TNA DEFE 5 72, Chiefs of Staff (56) 412, 19 November 1956.
2. TNA ADM 116 6209, Naval Report on Operation Musketeer, Vice Admiral M Richmond.
3. RMM, 3 Commando Brigade Report.
4. TNA ADM 116 6209 Naval Report.
5. RM M, 3 Commando Brigade Report.
6. TNA ADM 116 6209, Naval Report, sect 10.
7. Ibid sects 30-32.
8. Jackson & Bramall, *The Chiefs* p 298.
9. TNA DEFE 5 72, Chiefs of Staff Committee (56) 412, 19 November 1956, Problems arising from Operation Musketeer.
10. TNA ADM 116 6102, CinC Mediterranean Report, sect 15.

11. TNA AIR 20 10746, FOAC Report of Proceedings, sect 60.
12. TNA ADM 116 6209, Summary of Conclusions 6, 24.
13. FAAM, 63 CBGL sect report, HMS *Eagle*.
14. FAAM, Message from First Sea Lord to Captain H C D Maclean DSC RN, HMS *Eagle*, 1 January 1957.
15. TNA ADM 1 26666, Logistical Support and Military Planning.
16. TNA DEFE 5 72, Chiefs of Staff Committee (56) 412.
17. IWM P68, Vice Admiral G B Sayer Report on Operation Musketeer (Medical Dept).
18. TNA ADM 53 144486, log HMS *Manxman* November 1956, Captain Tibbits' enclosure.
19. TNA ADM 116 6136, sect 4, 395(a).
20. ADM 116 6209, Naval Report, sect 14.
21. Ibid, sect 395(e).
22. TNA WO 32 16731, Lessons Arising from Operation Musketeer.
23. Ibid.
24. TNA ADM 116 6136, sect 385, AWS Report of Proceedings.
25. TNA ADM 116 6136, Naval Report, CinC Mediterranean, Conduct of Operations, sect 374.
26. Naval Review Vol XLV No 1 January 1956, p 66.
27. Parliamentary Papers, Vol 558 col 1909, 3 November 1956.
28. TNA WO 32 16731, Lessons
29. Parliamentary Papers 1956/1957 Vol 566 Cols 211-212.
30. TNA AIR 1940, General Keightley Despatch, sect 11.
31. TNA MT 40 187, Appendix J.

Glossary

ACT	Air Control Team
AWS	Amphibious Warfare Squadron
Cabrank	Standing patrol of aircraft available, when called upon, for ground support.
CAP	Combat Air Patrol
CBGLS	Carrier Borne Ground Liaison Section (known as 'Ceeballs'.
CinC	Commander-in-Chief
CMS	Coastal Minesweeper
FOAC	Flag Officer Aircraft Carriers.
JHU	Joint Helicopter Unit
LCA	Landing Craft Assault
LCT	Landing Craft Tank
LSH	Landing Ship Headquarters
LST	Landing Ship Tank
LVT	Landing Vehicle Tracked
LZ	Landing Zone
MTB	Motor Torpedo Boat (sometimes referred to in documents as an E-boat).
NATO	North Atlantic Treaty Organisation
NOIC	Naval Officer in Charge
RAS	Replenishment At Sea.
RASC	Royal Army Service Corp
RFA	Royal Fleet Auxiliary
TF	Task Force
TH	Task Group
UNEF	United Nations Emergency Force
USSR	Union of Soviet Socialist Republics
Z	Greenwich Mean Time, e.g. 0900Z.

Index

PERSONNEL

INDEX OF SHIPS ENGAGED IN OPERATION MUSKETEER AND ITS AFTERMATH.

As so many ships took part, they are normally listed if they are referred to more than once in the text. There are exceptions.